641.594 Sko
Skowronek, Julia
Oktoberfest cookbook

$20.00
ocn900180407
First American   09/23/2015

Oktoberfest Cookbook

Julia Skowronek

Oktoberfest Cookbook

With photographs by
Brigitte Sporrer

Contents

A festival of opposites — 7

From royal wedding to the world's largest folk fair — 8

Snacks & soups — **11**

What to wear: traditional dress — 22

A guide to the large beer tents — 30

Entrées — **41**

A showcase for Munich beer — 50

Oktoberfest food: from roast to strudel — 52

Two turbulent weeks: Oktoberfest highlights — 68

Vegetarian & side dishes — **81**

Oktoberfest attractions: Hang on tight and don't let go! — 90

Oktoberfest etiquette — 108

Sweet treats & baked goods — **115**

Where, when, what, how: a brief visitors' guide to the fair — 138

A phrase guide to beer-tent Bavarian — 140

Index — 142

A festival of opposites

What's so fascinating about the Oktoberfest? If you want an answer, you will find it by strolling through the Theresienwiese ("Wiesn" for short), ideally in the early afternoon when the autumn sun shines brightly and the crowds are still manageable. You will encounter people who could not be more different. There will be young girls in brightly colored neon mini-dirndl skirts, teenage boys wearing T-shirts with slogans and hats shaped like beer mugs, people in creative and unusual costumes, and older married couples in traditional dress, or "Tracht'ngwand." A brief peek into the Hofbräu tent reveals that this is the place where most of the visitors from Australia, North America, and New Zealand gather. Here—earlier than in the other tents—the party atmosphere reaches its peak. But no matter which of the 14 large beer tents you find yourself in, by evening people will certainly be up on the benches—dancing, singing, and celebrating!

Many and varied

Outside the tents, the aromas of roasted chicken and fish grilled on a stick ("Steckerlfisch") mingle with those of cotton candy and roasted almonds. Stalls invite the romantically inclined to buy heart-shaped cookies. Nearby, people are throwing balls at cans, trying to topple them—more or less successfully. In the beer garden in front of the Fischer-Vroni tent, things are more relaxed. An older couple sits and enjoys a beer and grilled fish; they have come to the fair every year for more than 40 years. Suddenly, resounding shrieks disturb the peaceful atmosphere: A few fearless (or perhaps not so fearless) thrill-seekers plunge downward 265 feet (80 meters) from the Skyfall-Turm platform.

Young and old, modern and traditional—how does this all work? How harmonious is the Oktoberfest? The Bavarian answer is "passt scho!" or "it all goes together just fine!" Since its beginning, the largest folk fair in the world has been innovative and modern, yet visitors can also experience traditional values, the glory of the past, and a relaxed and welcoming atmosphere. It is a lovely contradiction that attracts such a wide variety of visitors every year.

In food paradise

Given all the spectacle, one aspect of the Oktoberfest might not be so obvious. It isn't all about drinking beer here; it's also about eating really well. Even some of the local visitors from the region aren't aware just how wide the Oktoberfest's culinary range is beyond the classic grilled chicken. Bavarian delicacies of all kinds are sold in both the large tents and in the increasingly popular smaller tents, at countless food stalls, and in the more traditional restaurants of the "Old Fair." The food ranges from roasted ox to fish sandwiches, from game to vegan, from sour lungs to sweet fruit dipped in chocolate. Somewhere among the many choices you will discover your personal Oktoberfest favorite.

Inspired by this culinary bounty, we have gathered together the tastiest, most popular, and most traditional Bavarian Oktoberfest recipes. Let this collection of recipes serve as your culinary tour guide. Discover your favorite beer tent and drink. Celebrate at the festival, enjoy the food, and re-create it in your own kitchen. Or, if you can't get to the actual festival, just bring that Oktoberfest feeling into your home. Serve a mouth-watering selection of bread, sausage, and cheese, or a hearty soup, a sophisticated roast, and a homemade dessert as you celebrate with friends and family at your very own private Oktoberfest party.

From royal wedding to the world's largest folk fair

The Oktoberfest has its roots in a jubilant royal wedding. On October 12, 1810, Crown Prince Ludwig, later King Ludwig I of Bavaria, married Princess Therese. The festival lasted for five days, and the young kingdom seized the opportunity to show off its brightest and best. The city of Munich was filled with festival events, parades, food and drink, musicians, and curiosities. A horse race topped the bill on a meadow named in honor of the bride, and this is what the locals have nicknamed the Oktoberfest: the "Wiesn"—short for Theresienwiese—or "Therese's meadow." The fair was so well received that it was decided to hold it annually, and the Oktoberfest tradition was born. The horse races quickly had competition from other attractions. First came the carousels and giant swings, then roller coasters and haunted houses, variety shows, curiosity cabinets, shooting stands, and games of chance. But even almost 200 years ago, what drew the locals to the Theresienwiese was the beer—specifically, the Munich beer. For then, as is the case today, only traditional Munich breweries were allowed to serve the specially brewed festival beer.

Soon, more visitors streamed to the fairgrounds. To cope with the crowds, the first giant tents were set up at the end of the 19th century. One by one, these replaced the many small beer stalls. Michael Schottenhamel opened the first beer tent in 1867 behind the King's tent. Every year, Munich's mayor still officially launches the festival in the Schottenhamel tent by tapping the first keg of beer and calling out *"O'zapft is!"*—"it is tapped."

History of the fair

1810 The marriage of the Bavarian Crown Prince Ludwig and Therese von Sachsen-Hildburghausen was celebrated with a folk fair.

1818 Beer was served at the fair for the first time.

1835 On the occasion of his silver wedding anniversary, King Ludwig I held a parade of people in historic traditional costume. This was the precursor of today's traditional costume parade.

1850 The Bavaria, a gigantic statue symbolizing the land of Bavaria, was dedicated overlooking the Theresienwiese.

1872 The start of the Oktoberfest was moved earlier—to September—due to bad weather.

1880 The Oktoberfest was electrified. Around 400 drink and food concessions and fair stalls shone in the luster of electric light.

1919 The first swing carousel, the "Kettenflieger Kalb," started operation.

1950 For the first time, the Oktoberfest was opened with a festive beer barrel tapping by the Mayor of Munich, Thomas Wimmer, with the famous call *O'zapft is!*

2010 The Oktoberfest had its 200th anniversary. Part of the Theresienwiese was set aside to celebrate the Oktoberfest tradition with nostalgic festival tents and old-fashioned rides. The "Old Fair" has since become a permanent feature of the Oktoberfest.

Snacks & soups

Brotzeit platter with cheese, cold meats, radish, and more

A handsomely arranged cold meat and cheese platter or "Brotzeit" makes the perfect start to a successful Oktoberfest evening. It is accompanied by pretzels and, of course, a refreshing beer.

Serves 4 · Prep time: 30 minutes

For the platter
- 1 daikon radish
- 1 bunch of radishes
- 4 landjäger sausages or salami (about 1lb)
- 3½oz (100g) smoked ham, sliced
- 3½oz (100g) Swiss cheese, sliced
- 2 tbsp chopped chives
- salt, pepper

For the Camembert spread
- 7oz (200g) Camembert cheese
- 7oz (200g) ricotta, cottage, cream, or other fresh cheese
- salt, pepper
- 1 tbsp paprika
- 2 red onions
- 1 handful of salted pretzels

For the radish spread
- 1 bunch of radishes
- 14oz (400g) ricotta, cottage, or cream cheese
- salt, pepper
- 1 squeeze of fresh lemon juice

For the arugula spread
- 2 bunches of arugula
- 14oz (400g) ricotta, cottage, or cream cheese
- salt, pepper
- 1 squeeze of fresh lemon juice

1. To prepare the platter, slice the daikon radish very thinly. Use a spiralizer if you have one. Keeping the radishes bunched together, wash them thoroughly and leave to drain. Cut the sausages in half.

2. To make the cheese spread, break the Camembert into small pieces with a fork. Add the fresh cheese and combine. Season the spread with salt, pepper, and paprika. Peel the onions and slice them into rings.

3. To make the cheese and radish spread, coarsely chop the radishes. Stir into the fresh cheese and season with salt, pepper, and lemon juice.

4. To make the cheese and arugula spread, coarsely chop the arugula. Add to the fresh cheese and combine. Season the spread with salt, pepper, and lemon juice.

5. Place the sliced daikon radish in the center of a large wooden platter. Arrange the bunched radishes, landjäger or salami, ham, Swiss cheese, and the three cheese spreads around the radish. Garnish the Camembert spread with onion rings and salted pretzels. Scatter chopped chives over the entire platter and serve with salt and pepper on the side. Freshly-baked pretzel cheese sticks, snails, and chestnuts (see p. 113), farmer's bread, and pretzels go well with this dish.

Tip: This platter can be varied to taste. For example, you can use any kind of air-cured or cooked sausage, homemade liverwurst (see p. 15), dill pickles, cold slices of roast suckling pig (see p. 47), boiled ham hocks (see p. 44), Oktoberfest chicken (see p. 74), or grünkern (spelt) patties (see p. 94). Open-faced chive sandwiches are also delicious on a Brotzeit platter. To make these, butter slices of farmer's bread, then press the buttered sides into the chopped chives.

Snacks & soups 15

Homemade liverwurst
with nutmeg and marjoram

Why not try making liverwurst yourself? It's easier than you think, and you'll know what's in it, too. Decorated with a blue-and-white label, a jar of liverwurst makes a great little gift to bring to any Oktoberfest party.

Makes 6 screw top jars (7fl oz/200ml each) · Prep time: 1 hour · Cooking time: 1 hour · Processing time: 1 hour · Keeps for 6 months

1lb 2oz (500g) pork belly with rind
1lb 2oz (500g) pork meat (such as neck, leg, shoulder)
1lb 2oz (500g) pork liver
salt
2 onions
1 tbsp vegetable oil
pepper
2 pinches of grated nutmeg
1 tbsp dried marjoram

You will also need
a meat grinder
6 sterilized jars, holding 7fl oz (200ml) each, and sterilized self-sealing lids to match

1 Coarsely chop the pork belly, meat, and liver. Cover the liver and put it into the refrigerator. In a large pot, bring a generous amount of salted water to a boil. Place the chopped pork belly and meat into the water, reduce the heat, and cook for about 1 hour or until tender. Remove the meat with a slotted spoon, reserve the broth, and leave both to cool.

2 Peel the onions and chop them coarsely. Heat the oil in a pan, add the onions, and sauté. Remove from the heat and leave to cool.

3 Using a fine grinder plate (about 3/16in (4mm)), put the liver, cooked pork, and cooked onions through a meat grinder. Repeat. Pour 7fl oz (200ml) of the reserved broth over the liverwurst mixture and mix thoroughly. Season the mixture liberally with salt, pepper, nutmeg, and marjoram. Pour the mixture into the sterilized jars, packing them no more than three-quarters full. Seal with the sterilized lids.

4 Use a pressure canner to eliminate the risk of contamination, following the manufacturer's instructions. Serve the liverwurst on a Brotzeit platter.

Tip: You can vary the liverwurst recipe to taste. For example, try adding 2 stewed, cubed apples, or 1 tablespoon of chopped flat-leaf parsley and 1 tablespoon of chopped chives, or 3 tablespoons of cooked cranberries to the meat mixture. Another delicious variation is to substitute 2 tablespoons of coarsely chopped pistachios for the marjoram.

Mixed salad
with deep-fried Camembert

In this dish, fresh, crunchy lettuce leaves and crisp fried cheese come together on a plate—a real treat from Oktoberfest heaven. It is no wonder that this simple dish has so many fans.

Serves 4 · Prep time: 40 minutes

For the salad
1 apple
1 handful of cherry tomatoes
1 bunch of radishes
2 carrots
4 handfuls of mixed lettuce leaves
salt, pepper
3 tbsp vinegar
¼ cup vegetable oil

For the fried Camembert
4 Camembert rounds (5½oz/150g each)
3 eggs
2 tbsp all-purpose flour
breadcrumbs, for coating
oil, for frying
¼ cup lingonberry or cranberry compote (from the jar), to serve

1. To make the salad, core and slice the apple, leaving the peel on. Cut the cherry tomatoes in half. Slice the radishes. Peel and coarsely grate the carrots. Add the apple, tomatoes, radishes, and carrots to the lettuce, and toss.

2. Combine the salt, pepper, vinegar, and oil to make a dressing. Set aside until serving time.

3. To make fried Camembert, cut each Camembert round into quarters. Whisk the eggs in a deep plate or bowl. Put the flour and breadcrumbs each on separate plates.

4. Dip each piece of Camembert into the flour and shake off the excess. Then dip each piece into the whisked eggs, and finally into the breadcrumbs. Press the breadcrumbs firmly into the cheese and shake off any excess. Dip the cheese wedges into the egg and then the breadcrumbs a second time.

5. Heat up a generous amount of oil in a shallow pan. Working in batches, fry the pieces of Camembert in the hot oil for about 5 minutes, or until they are crisp on the outside. Remove and let drain on paper towels.

6. Add the dressing to the salad, toss, and portion out onto four plates. Working quickly, place four pieces each of fried Camembert on top. Serve the compote on the side.

# Sausage salad—three ways

To make the dressing
- salt, pepper
- ¼ cup sherry vinegar
- ¼ cup dill pickle juice (from the jar) or vegetable broth
- ¼ cup vegetable oil

Serves 4 each · Prep time: 20 minutes each

1. Combine the salt, pepper, vinegar, dill pickle juice, and oil to make a dressing. Set aside until serving time.

Bavarian sausage salad

- 1lb 5oz (600g) cooked deli sausage, such as Regensburg, beerwurst, ham or turkey kielbasa, or bologna sausage
- 4 dill pickles (from the jar)
- 2 red onions

1. Remove the sausage casings. Thinly slice the sausage and the dill pickles. Peel the onions and slice them into thin rings. Put all the ingredients in a serving bowl.

2. Drizzle the dressing over the sausage, pickles, and onions, and toss. Leave the salad to marinate for about 15 minutes before serving.

Swiss sausage salad

- 14oz (400g) leberkaese; alternatively, cooked deli sausage such as bierwurst, mortadella, ham or turkey, kielbasa, or bologna sausage
- 7oz (200g) Swiss cheese
- 1 bunch of radishes

1. Cut the sausage and Swiss cheese into thin strips. Trim and wash the radishes, and wash the radish greens. Slice the radishes and coarsely chop the greens. Put the sausage, Swiss cheese, and radish slices in a serving bowl.

2. Drizzle the dressing over the salad and toss. Leave the salad to marinate for about 15 minutes. Add the radish greens, toss again, and serve immediately.

Tart head cheese

- 4 slices red head cheese (3oz/80g each)
- 8 slices white head cheese (1½oz/40g each)
- 2 onions
- 2 dill pickles (from the jar)

1. Arrange the slices of red and white head cheese on four plates and drizzle with the dressing. Leave to marinate for about 15 minutes.

2. Peel the onions and slice them into rings. Cut the pickles in half lengthwise, make lengthwise cuts into each half, and fan out. Top the slices of head cheese with the onion rings and pickle, and serve.

Freshly smoked trout fillets

Smoking fish is really easy and very satisfying. You can even do it in your own kitchen. Using different types of sawdust, herbs, and spices, you can conjure up new flavors each time. Give it a try—but make sure to open your windows!

Serves 4 · Prep time: 30 minutes

2 bay leaves
4 sprigs of rosemary
4 sprigs of thyme
4 trout fillets, about 5½oz (150g) each, boneless, skin on
salt, pepper
1 piece of fresh horseradish, about 1½in (4cm) long

You will also need
1 large food-safe metal tin (such as a cookie tin)
3 handfuls of smoking sawdust
a cake rack or metal steamer rack to fit the tin

1. Using a large knife, screwdriver, or can opener, punch several holes into the lid of the tin.

2. Sprinkle the sawdust over the bottom of the tin. Break up the bay leaf and stir it into the sawdust, along with the rosemary and thyme. Sit the rack on the sawdust.

3. Season the fish fillets with salt and pepper and arrange them side by side, skin side down, on the cake rack. Close the tin and place it on the stove. Heat the tin over medium heat until smoke begins to rise out of the holes, then smoke the trout for about 10 minutes.

4. Meanwhile, finely grate the horseradish. When the fish is smoked, open the tin and remove the fillets. Sprinkle the grated horseradish over the smoked trout and serve.

Tip: You can reuse the tin several times. After you have smoked the fish, wash the tin, dry it thoroughly, and store it in a plastic bag.

What to wear: traditional dress

Dressing up to go to the Oktoberfest is a long-standing tradition, but the meaning of "dressing up" has changed dramatically since 1810. While lederhosen, or leather shorts, and dirndl are almost mandatory for today's fair, in the 1990s you wore jeans if you belonged to the fashionable mainstream. In contrast, at the start of the last century, the citizens dressed to the nines for a day at the fair—this meant tuxedos and top hats, or formal dresses. The dirndl has its origins in the traditional work clothes of maidservants and farmers' wives in the 19th century. Traditional costume and the Oktoberfest first came together in the 1960s, but only in the 21st century did traditional dress become the norm for visitors from around the world.

So how does one dress properly for the fair? Dirndls come in many styles, and the sturdy lederhosen, which were formerly the work clothes of farmers, come in various lengths and leathers. Here are the standards, which will help you get the look you want.

Traditional women's costume

No matter if she is young or old, plump or willowy—every woman can wear a dirndl. They flatter the figure, show off the waist and cleavage, and conceal a lot. The dress is always worn with an apron. The variety of colors, cuts, and patterns—flowers, stripes, checks, and more—is nearly never-ending; there's a style for every taste. The ideal Oktoberfest dirndl falls just below the knee. Traditionalists, however, prefer ankle-length skirts. And then there is the mini dirndl, which doesn't have much in common with the traditional dirndl. No matter the length, a dirndl is often paired with a blouse, usually white.

The festival outfit is complemented by a matching hairstyle. Braided hair and updos are especially popular. Those who don't want to make the effort or aren't nimble-fingered enough can have their hair braided or styled by a hairdresser. Don't forget to bring along a warm jacket to put on later—a traditional one if you want to be dressed in style—because you will feel the cold when you leave the beer tent.

Traditional men's costume

Men have a choice of leather shorts, which come in long, short, or knee-length styles. Depending on their budget and taste, men can choose lederhosen made from stag, mountain goat, goat, or cow leather, with yellow, green, or white embroidery, with suspenders or without. The most important thing is that they fit nice and snug, yet are comfortable to wear. Men with muscular calves wear "Loferl," or knitted calf warmers. Men with slender legs are better off donning the regular traditional socks. The leather shorts are worn with a traditional shirt—not a T-shirt—and a matching jacket.

Jewelry and shoes

Silver jewelry is worn discreetly with traditional costume. It is often adorned with rubies, mountain crystal, or pearls. The chains on the dirndl bodice are often decorated with mounted silver coins. A very special piece of jewelry is the charivari, a short silver chain that has hunting trophies, lucky charms, precious stones, or coins dangling from it. Women wear it on the dirndl bodice; men wear it on the waist of their shorts. You can't just buy a charivari—you have to acquire or earn it. You add charms over time before passing it on to the next generation.

And what about shoes? Pumps or elegant shoes with high, but not extravagantly high, heels go best with a dirndl. Make sure your shoes are comfortable—after all, you will have to wear them for several hours of dancing and celebrating. Besides comfort, you will also need to think about your safety—remember that glass beer mugs can easily drop and shatter.

For men, choosing shoes is a much simpler task. Only "Haferlschuh'," or traditional shoes, really go with leather shorts. If you don't have a pair of traditional shoes, you can wear hiking shoes instead.

The bow code

The bow on the apron reveals what kind of relationship the wearer is in:

Bow on the left—single
Flirting is allowed or even desired when the bow is on the left. If you aren't married, but you are in a relationship, where your bow is tied is between you and your conscience.

Bow at the back—widow
If people offer you condolences even though you're not a widow, you should probably check the bow at the back of your dirndl.

Bow on the right—taken
Traditionally only married women tied the bow on the right. However, anyone trying to avoid unwanted attention can take advantage of this trick.

Gravad lax sandwiches
with homemade cured salmon

The fair's snack and fish stalls offer a huge choice of fish sandwiches, but the "Lachssemmel"—gravad lax roll—remains the absolute classic.

Serves 4 · Prep time: 40 minutes · Brining time: 12 hours

1 organic lemon
½ cup salt
¾ cup sugar
½ tsp black peppercorns
1 salmon fillet, about 1lb 5oz (600g), boneless, and skin on
2 large eggs
1 red onion
4 sandwich rolls
butter, for the bread
2 tbsp chopped dill
1 handful of salad leaves

1 Slice the lemon. Stir together the salt, sugar, and black peppercorns. Sprinkle half the seasoning mixture into a deep casserole dish and arrange half of the lemon slices on top. Place the salmon fillet on top of the lemon, sprinkle over the remaining seasoning, and top with the remaining lemon slices. Cover the dish and put it in the refrigerator for 12 hours to brine.

2 Boil the eggs for about 8–10 minutes until hard-boiled. Rinse under cold running water; peel and slice the eggs. Peel the onion and slice into rings. Cut the rolls in half and butter the cut sides.

3 Remove the salmon from the brine, wash it in cold water, and pat dry. Then sprinkle the dill evenly over the salmon. Cut the fillet into very thin slices.

4 Arrange a few salad leaves on the cut side of the top half of each roll. Place several slices of gravad lax on the bottom half. Add a layer of onion rings and a layer of sliced egg on top of the salmon, cover with the top half of the roll, and serve immediately.

Tip: *There is another classic dish that provides emergency relief after a hard day at the fair—the Bismarck herring sandwich. To make it, slice 1 onion into rings and cut 2 dill pickles into slices. Cut open 4 sandwich rolls and layer each bottom half with 1 Bismarck herring fillet, slices of onion, and dill pickle. Replace the top half of the roll and enjoy!*

Snacks & soups

Matjes herring fillets
in a creamy apple-and-yogurt sauce

Chicken, hocks, sausages, duck, roast... with so much meat on offer, fresh matjes are a welcome change. One large beer tent at the fair has made fish dishes its specialty, including the classic "Steckerlfisch," fish grilled on a stick.

Serves 4 · Prep time: 20 minutes

1 onion
2 dill pickles (from the jar)
1 apple
salt
¼ cup mayonnaise
10½oz (300g) low fat, plain yogurt
¼ cup dill pickle juice (from the jar)
2 tbsp chopped dill
pepper
4–8 double matjes herring fillets, or mildly seasoned, pickled herring fillets from the jar, such as wine-marinated herring

1. Peel the onion and slice it into rings. Slice the dill pickles. Cut the apple into eight pieces. Remove the core and slice the apple, leaving the peel on.

2. Bring salted water to a boil in a pot. Blanch the onion slices in the boiling water, drain, and cool under cold running water or in ice water. When cool, set aside to drain.

3. Mix together the mayonnaise, yogurt, and dill pickle juice. Stir in the onion, pickles, sliced apple, and dill. Season the sauce with salt and pepper to taste.

4. Rinse the matjes fillets in cold water and pat them dry with paper towels. Portion out the sauce onto four plates and arrange a double herring fillet on each plate. Parslied potatoes (see p. 103) go well with this dish.

Tip: Fancy some color? Adding red beets will turn the sauce pink. Cook 2 medium red beets for about 45 minutes until tender, and leave to cool. Peel the beets, cut them into slices, and stir them into the apple-and-yogurt sauce. If you are in a hurry, use sliced red beets from the jar.

Autumnal squash soup
with pumpkin seed oil

What could be nicer than sitting outside in the afternoon and enjoying the autumn sun? You will have ample opportunity to do this during the Oktoberfest, before the cold season arrives. Squash soup is perfect right now!

Serves 4 · Prep time: 40 minutes

1 onion
¼ cup celery root, chopped
¼ cup carrots, chopped
1 cup leek, chopped
⅔ cup parsnip, chopped
4 sprigs of flat-leaf parsley
1 Hokkaido (red kuri) or butternut squash, about 1lb 10½oz (750g)
2 tbsp vegetable oil
3¼ cups vegetable broth
1 bay leaf
4 sprigs of thyme
2 tbsp pumpkin seeds
1 cup heavy cream
salt, pepper
1 pinch of grated nutmeg
2 tbsp pumpkin seed oil, for drizzling

1. Peel the onion and dice it coarsely. Coarsely chop the celery root, carrots, leek, parsnip, and parsley. Wash the squash, cut it in half, and scrape out and discard the seeds. Cut the squash into large pieces.

2. Heat the oil in a large pot, add the onion, and sauté. Stir in the remaining vegetables, the parsley, and the squash, and continue to sauté for about 5 minutes. Pour in the vegetable broth. Add the bay leaf and thyme. Bring everything to a boil, then reduce the heat and simmer for about 20 minutes, or until the vegetables are tender.

3. Meanwhile, toast the pumpkin seeds for about 3 minutes in a pan, stirring constantly. Set aside until serving time.

4. Remove the thyme and bay leaf from the soup. Using an immersion blender, purée the soup in the pot. Then return it to a boil, stir in the cream, and season with salt, pepper, and nutmeg.

5. Serve the soup in soup bowls, with pumpkin seeds scattered over the top and a drizzle of pumpkin seed oil.

A guide to the large beer tents

Which tent should I choose? For many fair visitors, this is crucial. You can spend a pleasant evening in one of the many small or medium-sized tents—but standing on benches singing and celebrating with thousands of other people in one of the large Oktoberfest tents is a truly amazing experience. There are 14 giant tents to choose from, each serving beer from a traditional Munich brewery, as well as wine. The tents differ in terms of atmosphere, decoration, clientele, and size. The tents' menus, too, may offer special dishes that could lead you to choose one tent over another.

Hit songs for having fun

Despite their differences, all the large tents have one thing in common: the bands who do their best to get the crowds going. The so-called "Oktoberfest hits," however—often well-known German songs or classic rock, pop, and country hits—can only be played after 6pm. Before then, it is quieter in all the tents, and the mood is more traditional. But as soon as the roasted chicken or ox has been consumed, the tempo increases, the breaks become shorter and less frequent, and the top hits—from "Fürstenfeld" to "Griechischer Wein"—are played one after the other, until everyone in the tent is on their feet.

Usually the evening's success depends on the service. A good waiter is the real manager of the tables at the Oktoberfest. The waiters keep an eye on their guests, are quick to bring the next round, and don't let you know when they're feeling stressed. The myth of the cranky Oktoberfest waiter persists, but today, friendly and attentive service is highly valued at the Oktoberfest. And your waiters will certainly be nice to you if you are nice to them. Respect and good manners are called for at the fair just like anywhere else. A generous tip never hurts, too.

Getting into the tents

The Oktoberfest is a magnet for millions. This means on weekends, and also some weekdays, the beer tents are often closed due to overcrowding. Only when one visitor leaves can someone else enter. There is no special trick, no convincing argument, plea, insult, or charm offensive that will convince the bouncers to let you in—after all, they've seen it all before.

If you want to be sure of getting a table in a tent, you should reserve early—because if you don't have a seat, you usually won't be served any beer! Tables can be reserved starting in January for the current year. Contact information, and/or information about how to reserve, is usually found on the website of the respective tent. Processing the requests is often a lengthy process, so don't give up. Companies who plan to invite their employees and/or customers to the

Oktoberfest also have to persist. Making a table reservation is free, but the reservation is tied to mandatory consumption of food and drink. In the best case scenario, you are required to purchase coupons for the value of two liters of beer and half a chicken per person, payable in advance. But it can, and often does, add up to significantly more than this.

Choosing the right tent

Which tent is the right one for me? Here are a few guidelines to help you decide. In the Augustiner, Armbrustschützen, Ochsenbraterei, and Winzerer Fähndl tents, the style is set by ideals of Bavarian "Gemütlichkeit," which roughly means a feeling of coziness and friendliness. In contrast, the wildest and most international parties are found in the Hofbräu and Löwenbräu tents. Here you will encounter the largest number of overseas visitors, including Australians, New Zealanders, and Americans. The crowd is slightly younger in the Schottenhamel, Schützen, and Hacker tents. The Hacker tent has been nicknamed "Bavarian Heaven" for its cheerful ceiling, prettily painted with clouds and stars. The Bräurosl is the meeting place for the gay community. The choice of tent can also be influenced by culinary considerations. If you want ox freshly roasted on a spit, head to the Ochsenbraterei. Anyone who would rather eat fish grilled on a stick should try Fischer-Vroni's tent or outdoor beer garden. In the opulently decorated Marstall tent, which features a large champagne bar, the atmosphere is much more dignified. Here—as well as in Kuffler's Weinzelt, which is dedicated to wine—the majority of the crowd is over the age of 30. And Käfer's gourmet tent is the place to mingle for the VIPs, the rich, and the beautiful, as well as their hangers-on.

Those who don't need all that hustle and bustle, and who would rather sit than stand on a bench, will feel more comfortable in the Tradition or the Herzkasperl tents at the more traditional "Old Fair," where popular bands from the Munich music scene also take the stage.

Hearty goulash
with Oktoberfest beer

With this goulash in your belly you will be perfectly prepared for the wildest rides and the fair's legendary variety show, "beim Schichtl." You will also survive the Teufelsrad and Toboggan rides without a scratch.

Serves 4 · Prep time: 35 minutes · Cooking time: 1 hour

1lb 2oz (500g) onions
oil, for frying
1lb 2oz (500g) boneless beef (such as leg, shoulder, shank), cut into small cubes
1 tbsp tomato paste
1 tbsp paprika
1 cup Oktoberfest beer
salt
1 tsp dried marjoram
1 tsp caraway seeds
zest of 1 organic lemon
1lb 2oz (500g) yellow potatoes, such as Yukon Gold
2 red bell peppers
fresh marjoram leaves, to garnish

1 Peel the onions and dice them finely. In a large pot, heat up a little oil. Add the diced onions and sauté. Add the cubes of beef and cook for about 10 minutes, or until the beef juices have completely evaporated.

2 Stir in the tomato paste and sprinkle the paprika over the meat. Pour in the beer to deglaze the pot, then add 3 cups of water. Season with salt, marjoram, caraway, and lemon zest, and bring to a boil. Now reduce the heat and simmer the goulash for about 1 hour, stirring occasionally.

3 Meanwhile, peel the potatoes. Remove the seeds and stems from the peppers. Coarsely dice the potatoes and peppers. Add the diced potatoes to the pot about 45 minutes into the cooking time and add the diced pepper about 5 minutes before the end of the cooking time.

4 Serve the goulash in deep soup bowls, sprinkled with fresh marjoram, to taste. Crusty farmer's bread goes well with this dish.

Clear chicken soup
with noodles and vegetables

Hot chicken soup with plenty of meat and noodles warms you through and makes you feel happy. This soup serves 6 people as a first course or 4 as a main course.

Serves 4–6 · Prep time: 40 minutes · Cooking time: 1 hour

1 chicken, about 2½lb (1.2kg)
salt
½ cup celery root
½ cup carrots
2 cups leek
1⅓ cups parsnip
8 sprigs of flat-leaf parsley
½ tsp black peppercorns
1 bay leaf
5½oz (150g) dried soup noodles or egg noodles
2 tbsp chopped parsley, to garnish

1. In a large pot, bring salted water to a boil and add the chicken (it should be just covered with water). Return the water to a rolling boil and boil the chicken for about 5 minutes. Skim off any foam that rises to the surface. Coarsely chop half the celery root, carrots, leek, parsnip, and all the sprigs of parsley. Add the chopped vegetables to the chicken, along with the parsley, peppercorns, and bay leaf. Simmer over low heat for about 50 minutes. Check the pot occasionally to make sure the chicken is always covered with liquid and add water as needed.

2. Meanwhile, dice the remaining vegetables. Cook the noodles in boiling salted water according to the package instructions. They should be soft but al dente. Drain the noodles and rinse under cold running water.

3. Remove the chicken from the broth and leave to cool. Pour the broth through a fine mesh sieve into another pot, then return to a boil.

4. Remove the skin from the cooked chicken. Take the meat off the bone and cut into bite-size pieces.

5. Add the diced vegetables to the broth and cook until tender but still firm to the bite. Just before serving, add the chicken and the noodles to the broth to warm them. Ladle into soup bowls, garnish with chopped parsley, and serve.

Liver dumpling soup
with chopped chives

Many an Oktoberfest meal begins with a hearty liver dumpling soup. But beware: it's best to order soups only at lunchtime. In the evening, when the waitress has to balance her tray through the packed beer tent, the soup bowls often arrive at your table half full.

Serves 4 · Prep time: 40 minutes

For the liver dumplings
4 day-old bread rolls
1 cup milk
7oz (200g) beef liver
1 onion
1 tbsp unsalted butter
2 large eggs
2 tbsp chopped flat-leaf parsley
salt, pepper
1 pinch of grated nutmeg
1 tsp dried marjoram
1 tsp zest of 1 organic lemon

To serve
4 cups beef broth (from boiled beef, see p. 57)
2 tbsp chopped chives

1. To make the liver dumplings, thinly slice the rolls and place the slices in a bowl. Boil the milk, pour it over the sliced rolls, and mix thoroughly. Leave to soak for about 15 minutes.

2. Meanwhile, chop the liver into small pieces and purée with a blender or food processor. Peel the onion and dice it finely. Melt the butter in a pan, add the onion, and sauté.

3. Thoroughly combine the liver, onion, eggs, and parsley with the bread-and-milk mixture. Season with salt, pepper, nutmeg, marjoram, and lemon zest.

4. In a shallow pot, bring salted water to a boil. Form dumplings the size of golf balls with the liver mixture and place them in the boiling water. Reduce the heat and poach the liver dumplings for about 15 minutes.

5. Meanwhile, bring the beef broth to a boil. Using a slotted spoon, remove the liver dumplings from the salted water and lower them into the hot broth. Ladle broth and dumplings into soup bowls, sprinkle with chopped chives, and serve.

Tip: The liver dumplings can also be served with sauerkraut (see p. 44). This instantly turns them into a main course.

Leek and potato soup
with pretzel croutons

Consider yourself lucky if you find this rich and tasty soup on the menu!

Serves 4 · Prep time: 40 minutes

For the soup
- 2 leeks
- 1 onion
- 1lb 5oz (600g) white potatoes, such as Russet potatoes
- ¼ celery root
- 2 tbsp vegetable oil
- 1 bay leaf
- 3¼ cups vegetable broth
- 1 cup heavy cream
- salt, pepper
- 1 pinch of grated nutmeg

For the croutons
- 2 day-old soft pretzels
- 2 tbsp unsalted butter

1. To make the soup, cut off the white part of 1 leek and reserve the green part. Peel the onion, potatoes, and celery root. Coarsely chop the vegetables and the white part of the leek. Thinly slice the entire second leek and the reserved leek green into rings, and set aside.

2. Heat the oil in a large pot, add the onion, and sauté. Add the potatoes, celery root, leek, and bay leaf and sauté for a few minutes. Pour in the vegetable broth and simmer over low heat for about 15 minutes. Remove the bay leaf and purée the soup in the pot, using an immersion blender. Return to a boil, stir in the cream, and season the soup with salt, pepper, and nutmeg, to taste.

3. Bring a pot of salted water to a boil. Add the sliced leek and blanch, then drain in a sieve, plunge into ice water, and set aside.

4. To make the croutons, slice the pretzels. Melt the butter in a pan, add the slices, and cook until golden brown, stirring constantly.

5. Stir the blanched leeks into the soup to warm them. Ladle the soup into soup bowls, scatter pretzel croutons over the top, and serve.

Tip: Pale cream soups have an especially lovely color if you only use light-colored soup vegetables such as onion, celery root, parsnip, and the white part of the leek.

Entrées

Pork schnitzel cordon bleu

Wiener schnitzel yet again? No, today for a change let's have a crisp pork schnitzel prepared cordon bleu style—filled with ham and cheese.

Makes 4 portions · Prep time: 30 minutes

8 thinly cut boneless pork loin chops, each about 3oz (80g)
salt, pepper
4 slices cooked ham
4 slices Swiss cheese
2 large eggs
2 tbsp all-purpose flour
breadcrumbs, for coating
vegetable oil, for frying
1 lemon, to serve

You will also need
toothpicks

1. Using a meat tenderizer, flatten each pork chop into a thin schnitzel and season with salt and pepper. Lay out 4 schnitzels side by side on a cutting board. Top each with 1 slice of ham, 1 slice of Swiss cheese, and a second schnitzel. Use toothpicks to pin together the two schnitzels and their filling.

2. Whisk the eggs in a deep plate or bowl. Put the flour and breadcrumbs each on a separate plate.

3. Dip both sides of each schnitzel into the flour and shake off the excess. Now dip both sides into the egg, and finally into the breadcrumbs. Press the breadcrumbs lightly into the schnitzels and shake off the excess.

4. In one large (or two small) pans, heat a generous amount of oil, enough so the schnitzels will float. Put the schnitzels in the hot oil and fry them on one side. As you are frying, gently shake the pan back and forth so that the oil flows over the schnitzels. When they are golden brown underneath, turn the schnitzels over and reduce the heat. Fry until golden brown, then let drain on paper towels.

5. Cut the lemon into quarters and serve the pork schnitzels with the lemon wedges. Potato and endive salad (see p. 110) goes well with this dish.

Variation: If you like your food more savory, fill each schnitzel with 1 slice of prosciutto and 1 slice of a blue cheese, such as Gorgonzola, to make a cordon rouge schnitzel.

Boiled ham hocks
on a bed of sauerkraut salad

In Munich and Bavaria salt-cured meat is called "Surfleisch," and at the fair, boiled ham hocks are "Surhaxn." Elsewhere in Germany, they are known as "Eisbein."

Serves 4 · Prep time: 20 minutes · Cooking time: 1 hour 30 minutes

For the ham hocks
salt
4 ham hocks (also called pork hocks or pork knuckles), pickled in brine
¼ cup chopped celery root
¼ cup chopped carrot
1 cup chopped leek
⅔ cup chopped parsnip
4 sprigs of flat-leaf parsley, chopped coarsely
½ tsp black peppercorns
1 bay leaf

To make the spiced sauerkraut
1 onion
1 tbsp vegetable oil
1lb 2oz (500g) sauerkraut
1¼ cup ham hock broth or vegetable broth
½ tsp black peppercorns
½ tsp juniper berries
1 clove
1 bay leaf
1 pinch of sugar
salt

1 In a large pot, bring salted water to a boil, enough to just cover the pickled hocks. Add the hocks and return the water to a rolling boil, then cook the meat for about 5 minutes. Using a slotted spoon, skim off any foam that rises to the surface. Reduce the heat and simmer the hocks for about 90 minutes. Make sure the meat is always covered with liquid and add more water as needed.

2 After half the cooking time—45 minutes—add the chopped vegetables and parsley, the peppercorns, and the bay leaf to the pot. Cook the hocks for another 45 minutes.

3 Meanwhile, prepare the spiced sauerkraut. Peel the onion and slice it into rings. Heat the oil in a pot, add the onion, and sauté. Add the sauerkraut and pour in the broth. Add the black peppercorns, juniper berries, clove, bay leaf, and sugar. Season the sauerkraut with salt, to taste, and simmer over low heat for about 20 minutes.

4 Remove the hocks from the broth. Strain the broth through a fine mesh sieve and reserve to use in another dish, such as in sauerkraut. Arrange the ham hocks and the spiced sauerkraut on a platter and serve. Classic mashed potatoes or parslied potatoes (see p. 103) go very well with this dish.

Tip: You can also cook the ham hocks and the sauerkraut together in one pot. Sauté the onion and add the sauerkraut, celery root, carrots, leek, parsley, and seasonings, as described above. Place the ham hocks on the sauerkraut and add enough water to completely cover them. Cook for about 90 minutes. Add water as needed to ensure the hocks are always covered with liquid.

Roast suckling pig
with onion stuffing

This delicious rolled pork loin roast comes with an aromatic onion stuffing and an intensely flavored beer-based sauce. But if you prefer simplicity, it is also wonderful without the stuffing.

Serves 6 · Prep time: 40 minutes · Cooking time: 2 hours

3 onions
1 tbsp vegetable oil
1 tsp dried marjoram
2½lb (1.2kg) loin of suckling pig, boneless, with skin and belly fat on (order from the butcher)
1 tbsp mustard
salt, pepper
1 tsp caraway seeds
¼ cup diced celery root
¼ cup diced carrot
1 cup diced leek
⅔ cup diced parsnip
4 sprigs of flat-leaf parsley, coarsely chopped
2 cups Oktoberfest beer

You will also need
kitchen twine

1. To make the filling, peel 2 onions and slice them into rings. Heat the oil in a pan and add the onions. Cook them for about 5 minutes, turning often. Season the onions with the marjoram, remove from the stove, and leave to cool.

2. Preheat the oven to 350°F (180°C). Lay the pork loin flat on a cutting board, skin side down. Spread the mustard over the loin, and season it with salt and pepper. Distribute the onions evenly over the meat. Starting at the thickest end, roll up the loin, and tie it with kitchen twine.

3. Season the pork loin all over with the salt, pepper, and caraway seeds, and place in a roasting pan. Peel the remaining onion and coarsely dice. Add the diced onion, celery root, carrot, leek, and parsnip, as well as the chopped parsley, to the roasting pan and pour in 1 cup of water.

4. Place the pork in the middle of the oven and roast it for about 2 hours. Baste the meat with the juices every 15 minutes. If the skin turns too dark or does not brown enough, reduce or increase the oven temperature. Add a little water as necessary. Toward the end of the roasting time, pour the beer over the pork.

5. Remove the pork loin from the roasting pan and keep warm. Pour the sauce through a fine mesh sieve into a pot and set aside briefly, then carefully spoon off all the fat that has risen to the surface. Return the gravy to a boil.

6. Carve the roast into thick slices, and serve with the gravy. Potato dumplings (see p. 104) and Bavarian cabbage (see p. 99) are classic sides for this dish.

Tip: If suckling pig is not commonly sold in your area, you can also make a classic roast pork by following this recipe, using the same ingredients and method: Instead of loin of suckling pig, use 2¼lb (1kg) of pork shoulder, skin on (have the butcher score the skin for you), season as described above, and roast the pork for about 2 hours. The roast will serve 4.

It's all about the sausage

Feel like having sausage today, but can't decide which one? Here's a rundown of the five most important Oktoberfest types. Weißwurst, by the way, is a genuine Munich specialty, traditionally eaten before noon.

Weißwurst

A mild-tasting white sausage made from veal and parsley (center image).
Put 2 veal sausages per person into boiling salted water, reduce the heat immediately, and poach the sausages gently for about 15 minutes. To remove the casing before eating, cut open the sausage lengthwise and remove the sausage meat. Pretzels and sweet mustard are a must.

Wollwurst

This sausage is similar to veal sausage, but has no casing (lower right).
Dip 1–2 wollwursts per person in milk, then fry them on each side in hot oil for about 10 minutes until browned. Gravy, such as roast suckling pork gravy (see p. 47), and potato salad (see p. 110) or classic mashed potatoes (see p. 103) go well with this type of sausage.

Milzwurst

A poached sausage made with pieces of spleen (above right).
Per person, fry 1–2 finger-thick slices of milzwurst on each side in hot oil for about 10 minutes until browned. Add a little gravy, to taste. Another delicious way of preparing them is to dip the slices into breadcrumbs and fry them just like pork schnitzel (see p. 43). Serve with potato and endive salad (see p. 110) and remoulade sauce (see p. 78), to taste.

Leberkaese

Finely-ground sausage meat baked in the oven (below left). A Bavarian specialty. Serve 1 thick slice of leberkaese per person, ideally freshly baked. You can also fry slices of leberkaese in hot oil on each side for about 5 minutes until browned. Fried eggs, fried onions (see p. 82), potato salad (see p. 110), and sweet mustard—always a must in Bavaria—go well with this.

Schweinswürstel

A sausage made from coarsely ground pork (above left).
Cook 4 pork sausages per person on the grill or in a frying pan in hot oil on each side for about 10 minutes until crispy. Serve with sauerkraut (see p. 44) and medium-hot mustard.

A showcase for Munich beer

The historic Oktoberfest was always a festival thrown by Munich citizens for Munich citizens. This is why only the six traditional Munich breweries are allowed to serve beer at the fair. Breweries located outside the city limits are not granted a license to serve their beer at the fair.

Oktoberfest beer

Oktoberfest beer is brewed especially for the fair by the Munich breweries. It's a bottom-fermented beer, like the classic Munich Hell, but with a higher alcohol content (about 6 percent by volume). Every Oktoberfest beer has its own character, but generally the beer has a slightly bitter, slightly malty taste, is not highly carbonated, and is easy to drink—leading to many a drinker's downfall!

The beer is brewed in accordance with the Munich "Purity Law" of 1487, which was extended in 1516 to the whole of Bavaria. It states that only barley (or malted barley), hops, and water are allowed to be used for brewing. The yeast necessary for fermentation was later added to the list of permitted ingredients.

The Mass (spoken properly with a short "a" sound) is both a measure of beer and the vessel it is served in. The pottery mugs commonly used at earlier Oktoberfests, known as "Keferloher," were long ago replaced by glass mugs. The guests benefit from this, since the clear glass mugs make it easier for guests to complain about mugs that have been "badly poured" (not filled up to the standard measure line).

The six traditional Munich breweries

The **Augustiner** brewery is the oldest Munich brewery. A brewery existed in the Augustinerkloster on the Neuhauser Gasse as early as 1328. The monastery pub was popular with the locals even then. At the start of the 19th century, the monastery and its brewery were secularized. In 1817, the brewery passed into private hands. Of the "big six," the Augustiner brewery is the only one still family-owned and still using traditional wooden barrels, called "Hirschen," to store the beer. This time-honored brew is sold in the Augustiner tent, in Fischer-Vroni, and in the Tradition tent in the historic section of the Oktoberfest, the Old Fair.

The precursor to the **Hacker-Pschorr** brewery opened in 1417 in the Sendlinger Straße, where the restaurant Altes Hackerhaus still exists today. With the marriage of Therese Hacker to Joseph Pschorr in 1793, a brewery dynasty was formed—the Hacker and Pschorr breweries were merged. At 5.8 percent by volume, the alcohol content is the lowest of all the Oktoberfest beers. You can drink it in the Hacker tent, in the Pschorr Bräurosl tent, and in the Herzkasperl tent at the Old Fair.

The history of the **Löwenbräu** brewery goes back to the late 14th century. One of the largest breweries in

19th-century Munich, it became a publicly traded company as early as 1872 and set up its headquarters in Nymphenburger Straße. Löwenbräu merged with Spaten and Franziskaner and has belonged, since 2004, to the AB InBev Group, which merged with Anheuser Busch in 2008 to become the world's largest brewery company. Löwenbräu Oktoberfest beer is served in the Löwenbräu tent and in the Schützen tent.

Paulaner beer can be traced back to 1634, when it was brewed in the monastery of the Pauline monks in the Neuhauser Straße. This makes it the "youngest" of all Munich beers. Paulaner has also become well-known for the "Starkbieranstich," the annual tapping of the first barrel of bock beer at the Nockherberg brewery in March. Paulaner's golden ale is served in the Armbrustschützen tent, Winzerer Fähndl, and Käfer's gourmet tent.

The **Spaten** brewery was first mentioned in a document in 1397 and has changed hands many times since. In 1807 it was bought by the Royal Court Brewer, Gabriel Sedlmayer. His initials can still be seen on the company logo, a white spade on a red background, designed in 1884. Until the 1890s, Spaten was Munich's largest brewery. Today it belongs to AB InBev, like Löwenbräu. The fair is officially opened in the Schottenhamel tent with the tapping of a barrel of Spaten. Spaten is also served in the Marstall and Ochsenbraterei.

The **Hofbräuhaus** was founded in 1589 during the reign of Herzog Wilhelm V von Bayern. It was located on Platzl, near Marienplatz, where the world-famous restaurant still stands. The brewery has been owned by the state of Bavaria since the 19th century. In 1896, the brewery moved to Haidhausen, and the restaurant was built where the brewhouse once stood. In 1988 yet another move, to a newer, larger brewery in München-Riem, became necessary. With an alcohol content of 6.3 percent, Hofbräu is the strongest Oktoberfest beer and is—of course—served in the Hofbräu tent.

Even if the trends at the fairgrounds change, one thing is certain: Beer gets a little more expensive every year. The Oktoberfest beer price is determined in advance and can vary slightly, depending on the venue. In 2014, the price crept over the 10-Euro mark for the first time. However, this does not affect the enjoyment of millions of visitors, or the popularity of Oktoberfest beer.

Oktoberfest food: from roast to strudel

The fair is famous for the delicious Munich beer that flows in huge quantities. But in order for the body to handle large quantities of beer, it needs a solid food base. Here, Bavarian cuisine has lots to offer. A good tent landlord (manager) is not just someone who taps the most beer, has control of their tent, and employs the best waiters. He or she must also ensure people like what is sent out to the tables on those big trays. Competition is fierce!

Delicious Oktoberfest classics

One of the fair's food staples is roasted chicken, along with culinary basics such as pork sausages, ham hocks, duck, various roasted meats, and cheese spaetzle. These dishes are found everywhere at the fair, but some favorites are only available in certain tents.

In the Ochsenbraterei (the "Oxen Grill"), oxen—about 90 of them over the course of an Oktoberfest—are roasted on the spit. The first ox was roasted on the Theresienwiese on a specially constructed spit in 1881. Just as in those days, the name and weight of the animal turning on the spit is written on a large board above the grill. An entire ox has much to offer hungry visitors. As you might expect, the Ochsenbraterei's menu boasts a large variety of meat dishes.

On the other hand, anyone who likes "Steckerlfisch," fish grilled on a stick, cannot ignore another institution: the Fischer-Vroni tent. Mackerel, char, salmon, trout, whitefish, and sea bass are grilled here. The fish are spitted on sticks, lined up in a long row, and grilled over an open fire. The best thing to go with grilled fish is a crisp pretzel—and a fresh mug of beer, of course.

For those craving culinary variety, a visit to the smaller festival tents will be rewarding. In the Kalbsbraterei, Munich Knödelei, or Wildstuben, for example, or in one of several time-honored establishments serving roasted chicken and duck, the owners develop their own special dishes and take great pride in the reputations they have built for themselves.

It isn't just meat-lovers who will find happiness at the fair. More and more fairgoers are vegetarians or vegans, and the food concession owners have adapted. For some time now, a variety of vegetarian dishes have

been sold in the tents—among them creamy wild mushroom stew (see p. 89), cheese spaetzle, and spinach spaetzle (see p. 82). And no longer do vegan fairgoers have to bring their own food; quite a few restaurateurs have long taken note of this trend and offer dishes such as soy medallions, vegan cheese spaetzle, or vegetable-and-potato burgers.

Sweet treats

Eating enough food is important at the fair—it can't be stressed enough. Hence, a sweet conclusion to your meal is essential. After all, who's counting calories at a fair? Strudel, Kaiserschmarrn (see p. 120 and p. 124), or donuts are just some of the irresistible temptations to try. For those who like simpler desserts, there are many stalls and kiosks selling chocolate-dipped fruit, candy apples, cotton candy, almond and pistachio nougat, or bags of candied almonds to warm your hands. You'll find sweet Oktoberfest treats to make starting on page 114.

Anyone who wants to enjoy the culinary side of the Oktoberfest in peace and quiet should go to the fair at lunchtime on weekdays. This is the quietest time, and it's much easier to find a free seat. Your wallet will thank you, too, because from Monday to Friday between 10am and 3pm, many establishments offer reasonably priced, daily changing lunch menus. On sunny days there is even a genuine beer-garden feeling in the air; the late summer sun shines benignly on you as a parting gift.

In a recent Oktoberfest, fairgoers consumed...

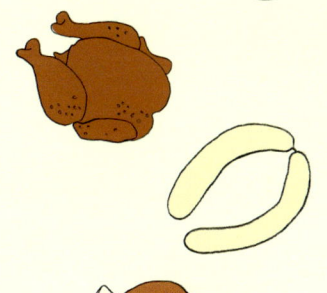

482,361 roasted chickens

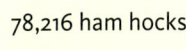

112,772 pairs of pork sausage

78,216 ham hocks

114 oxen and 85 calves

Stuffed breast of veal

This Bavarian classic is ideal for serving a large number of guests. What's special about it? This dish is main dish and side dish in one!

Serves 6 · Prep time: 50 minutes · Cooking time: 2 hours

1 portion of bread dumplings (see p. 104)
7oz (200g) cooked ham, diced
zest of ½ organic lemon
3⅓lb (1.5kg) trimmed boneless breast of veal, ready for stuffing (have the butcher make a pouch in the meat)
salt, pepper
2 tbsp vegetable oil
¼ cup diced celery root
¼ cup diced carrot
1 cup diced leek
⅔ cup diced parsnip
4 sprigs of flat-leaf parsley, chopped
1 bay leaf

You will also need
kitchen twine

1. Prepare the bread dumpling mixture as described on page 104. Add the diced ham and the lemon zest to the dumpling mixture and combine.

2. Preheat the oven to 350°F (180°C). Season the veal inside and out with salt and pepper. Stuff the dumpling mixture into the pouch and sew it up with kitchen twine.

3. Heat the oil in a roasting pan, add the breast of veal and brown it on all sides. Add the diced vegetables, chopped parsley, and bay leaf, and pour in about 3 cups of water. Roast the veal in the middle of the oven for about 2 hours, basting the meat now and then with the roasting juices. Add a little more water as necessary.

4. Remove the veal from the roasting pan and keep warm. Pour the roasting juices through a fine mesh sieve into a pot and bring to a boil. Carve the stuffed breast into thick slices and serve with the juices. A mixed salad is good with this.

Tip: If you are expecting more guests, you can buy a larger piece of veal—just ask your butcher for advice. No matter whether you buy a large or small piece, have the butcher prepare it for you by cutting a pouch in the meat.

Boiled beef
with fresh horseradish

This Bavarian treat is always popular, not just during the Oktoberfest. Boiled beef, called "Tellerfleisch" in Bavaria, can be prepared fairly effortlessly at home, and the resulting broth can be served as a delicious soup.

Serves 4 · Prep time: 40 minutes · Cooking time: 2 hours

To make the boiled beef
salt
2¼lb (1kg) boneless beef (chuck or shoulder)
½ tsp black peppercorns
1 bay leaf
8 sprigs of flat-leaf parsley, chopped
½ cup chopped celery root
½ cup chopped carrot
2 cups chopped leek
1⅓ cups chopped parsnip

To serve
2 tbsp chopped chives
¼ cup freshly grated horseradish
4 dill pickles (from the jar)

1. In a large pot, bring salted water to a boil, enough to just cover the beef. Add the beef and cook at a rolling boil for 5 minutes. Using a slotted spoon, skim off any foam that rises to the surface. Reduce the heat and simmer for about 2 hours. Add water as necessary to ensure the meat is always covered with liquid.

2. About 45 minutes before the end of the cooking time, add the peppercorns, bay leaf, parsley, and half of the chopped vegetables to the pot.

3. When the cooking time is up, remove the boiled beef from the pot and keep warm. Pour the broth through a fine mesh sieve into a second pot and return it to a boil. Add the rest of the chopped vegetables and simmer in the broth until tender but still firm.

4. Carve the beef into finger-thick slices. Arrange the slices of beef and vegetables on soup plates and pour a ladle of broth over each plate. Sprinkle with chives and serve with horseradish and dill pickles on the side.

Tip: Out of one dish, make two: in no time at all, the remaining broth is transformed into an exceptional beef soup with noodles. To make this soup, cook 5½oz (150g) of dried soup noodles in boiling salted water, following the directions on the package. Drain the noodles and reheat them in the broth along with ¼ cup of cubed boiled beef. Sprinkle with 2 tablespoons of chopped chives and serve.

Tender sauerbraten
in red wine sauce

Tender, braised beef with tasty gravy always makes a special meal!

Serves 4 · Prep time: 30 minutes · Cooking time: 2 hours · Marinating time: 3 days

- 2¼lb (1kg) boneless bottom round
- 1 onion, peeled and diced
- ¼ cup diced celery root
- ¼ cup diced carrots
- 1 cup diced leek
- ⅔ cup diced parsnip
- 4 sprigs of flat-leaf parsley, chopped
- 5 black peppercorns, coarsely crushed
- 1 tsp allspice
- 4 juniper berries, coarsely crushed
- 2 cloves
- 2 bay leaves
- 1 tsp mustard seeds
- 2 cups red wine
- ½ cup red wine vinegar
- salt, pepper
- 2 tbsp vegetable oil
- 2 tbsp all-purpose flour
- 1 tbsp tomato paste

1 Put the beef, the diced vegetables, the chopped parsley, and the spices into a bowl. Add the red wine and red wine vinegar, cover the meat, and leave to marinate in the refrigerator for at least 3 days, turning occasionally. Make sure the meat is always covered with liquid; if it is not, add a little more red wine.

2 Preheat the oven to 350°F (180°C). Remove the meat from the marinade and season it all over with salt and pepper. Strain the marinade through a sieve set over a bowl and reserve the liquid. Set aside the vegetables and spices left in the sieve.

3 Heat the oil in a roasting pan on the stove. Add the beef, brown it on all sides, and remove. Add the vegetables and spices. Sauté, then sprinkle with flour and stir in the tomato paste. Now pour in the reserved marinade, bring it to a boil, and return the meat to the pan. Place the roast in the middle of the oven and braise for 2 hours, turning it occasionally. Add a little water if necessary.

4 Remove the roast from the roasting pan and keep it warm. Pour the roasting juices through a fine mesh sieve into a pot and briefly return to a boil. Cut the sauerbraten into finger-thick slices and arrange on four plates with the sauce. Spaetzle (see tip p. 82) and red cabbage (see p. 99) make good sides for this dish.

Beef roulades
stuffed with dill pickles and bacon

Roulades are a classic lunch dish at the fair. They are accompanied by a mug of alcohol-free Mass, or a "Radler"—half beer and half lemon soda.

Serves 4 · Prep time: 50 minutes · Cooking time: 1 hour

1 Peel 2 of the onions and slice them into rings. In a pan, heat 1 tablespoon of oil and cook the bacon in it. Remove and let drain on paper towels. Add the onion rings to the pan and cook for about 5 minutes. Season with salt, pepper, and marjoram, and set aside to cool.

2 Lay out the pieces of beef side by side on a cutting board, spread each piece with mustard, and season with salt and pepper. Distribute the bacon, cooked onions, and pickles over the pieces of meat, leaving a clear edge about the width of a finger all the way around each piece. Turn in the edges, roll up the roulades, and secure with toothpicks.

3 Peel the remaining onion and coarsely dice. In a large pot, heat the remaining oil, add the roulades, and brown them on all sides. Remove from the pot and set aside. Now add the onion and other diced vegetables to the pot and sauté. Sprinkle in the flour and stir in the tomato paste, then add the red wine to deglaze the pot, and add 3 cups of water. Add the chopped parsley and bay leaf, and bring to a boil. Return the roulades to the pot and simmer in the sauce over low heat for about 1 hour, stirring now and then. Season with salt and pepper. If the sauce has reduced too much while the roulades are cooking, add a little more water.

4 Lift the roulades out of the pot and keep warm. Pour the sauce through a fine mesh sieve into a second pot and return briefly to a boil. Serve the roulades with the sauce and either classic mashed potatoes (see p. 103) or spaetzle (see tip p. 82).

3 onions
3 tbsp vegetable oil
3½oz (100g) smoked bacon, cut into strips
salt, pepper
1 tsp dried marjoram
4 pieces of boneless bottom round beef, about 7oz (200g) each, pounded to ¼in (6mm)
2 tbsp mustard
2 dill pickles (from the jar), cut into strips
¼ cup diced celery root
¼ cup diced carrots
1 cup diced leek
⅔ cup diced parsnip
2 tbsp all-purpose flour
1 tbsp tomato paste
5fl oz (150ml) red wine
4 sprigs of flat-leaf parsley, coarsely chopped
1 bay leaf

You will also need
toothpicks

Tip: *Is the meat done yet? One quick way of testing for doneness is to insert a skewer into the roulades (or the roast) at the end of the cooking time. If there is no resistance, the meat is cooked. If there is, cook for another 15 minutes and repeat the test.*

… Entrées

Lung stew

This dish might seem a little unusual to non-Bavarians. But try it, and you will be pleasantly surprised. Served with bread dumplings, it is an affordable lunch dish popular with many Oktoberfest visitors.

Serves 4 · Prep time: 45 minutes · Marinating time: 8 hours

5 black peppercorns, crushed
1 tsp allspice
4 juniper berries, crushed
2 bay leaves
1 tsp mustard seeds
3¼ cups vegetable broth
5fl oz (150ml) sherry vinegar
½ organic lemon, sliced
salt, pepper
1 pinch of sugar
1lb 2oz (500g) cooked lungs (from calf, cow, or pig), cut into strips
1 onion
2 tbsp clarified unsalted butter
2 tbsp all-purpose flour
2 tbsp chopped parsley, to garnish

1. Put the spices in a paper coffee filter or a piece of cheesecloth and tie with kitchen twine. Pour the vegetable broth into a pot, add the vinegar, spice sachet, and lemon slices, and bring to a boil. Season with salt, pepper, and sugar, remove from the stove, and set aside to cool.

2. Place the cooked lungs into the cooled liquid. Cover and marinate them in the refrigerator for at least 8 hours.

3. Strain the lungs through a sieve set over a bowl, reserving the marinade. Discard the spice sachet and the lemon slices.

4. Peel the onion and dice it finely. Heat the clarified butter in a large pot, add the diced onion, and sauté until golden brown. Dust with flour and cook until the onion is dark-gold in color, stirring constantly. Pour in the marinade all at once and continue stirring while it comes to a boil. Then reduce the heat and simmer the sauce for about 10 minutes, stirring frequently.

5. Add the marinated lungs to the sauce and simmer over low heat for about 10 minutes. Serve the lung stew in soup bowls, sprinkled with parsley. Bread dumplings (see p. 104) are very good with this dish.

Tip: Cooked lungs cut into thin strips are sold in practically every butcher shop in Bavaria. If cooked lungs are not available in your area, see if your butcher can order raw lungs, also known as lights, and cook them yourself. Wash the lungs, then peel and coarsely chop 1 onion. Bring a large pot of salted water to a boil, add the lungs, the onion, and 1 or 2 bay leaves, and simmer for about 2 hours, or until the lungs are tender. Lift out of the pot, remove any veins and gristle, and slice into very thin strips. The lungs now are ready to be used.

Venison stew

in juniper and red wine sauce

Hear those hunting horns? During the Oktoberfest, the hunting season for venison is in full swing in Bavaria, and there are many delicious game dishes to be enjoyed at the fair.

Serves 4 · Prep time: 40 minutes · Cooking time: 1 hour

2¼lb (1kg) stewing venison
salt, pepper
2 tbsp vegetable oil
1 onion, peeled and diced
¼ cup diced celery root
¼ cup diced carrot
1 cup diced leek
⅔ cup diced parsnip
2 tbsp all-purpose flour
1 tbsp tomato paste
7fl oz (200ml) red wine
4 sprigs of flat-leaf parsley, chopped
1 tsp juniper berries
1 bay leaf
2 cloves
½ tsp black peppercorns
7oz (200g) sour cream, to serve

1. Season the meat with salt and pepper. Heat the oil in a large pot, add the meat, and brown it on all sides. Remove from the pot and set aside.

2. Add the diced onion, celery root, carrot, leek, and parsnip to the pot and sauté in the remaining oil. Dust the vegetables with the flour and stir in the tomato paste. Add the red wine to deglaze the pot, then add 4 cups of water. Put the meat, parsley, juniper berries, bay leaf, cloves, and black peppercorns in the pot. Bring everything to a boil, reduce the heat, and simmer for about 1 hour, stirring occasionally. If the liquid reduces too much, add a little water.

3. Using a slotted spoon and tongs, lift the meat out of the sauce and set aside. Pour the sauce through a fine mesh sieve into a second pot and bring to a boil. Add the meat to the sauce to reheat.

4. Serve each portion of stew with a dollop of sour cream on top. Spaetzle (see tip p. 82) and red cabbage (see p. 99) go well with venison stew.

Tip: Poached pear halves filled with cranberry sauce make an excellent accompaniment for venison stew. Peel 2 pears, cut them in half, and remove the cores. Put 1¼ cup white wine or water in a pot, add 1 tablespoon of sugar and ½ cinnamon stick, and bring to a boil. Put the pears in the poaching liquid (the pears should be just covered) and simmer over low heat for about 10 minutes. Remove the pears with a slotted spoon and fill each pear half with 1 tablespoon of cranberry or lingonberry compote (from the jar). If you are in a hurry, use canned pear halves.

Braised lamb shanks
on root vegetables

Slowly braised lamb shanks are a lighter alternative to the rich roast ham hocks. A freshly-poured mug of Oktoberfest beer goes well with this.

Serves 4 · Prep time: 35 minutes · Cooking time: 1 hour

4 lamb shanks
   (10½oz/300g each)
salt, pepper
3 tbsp vegetable oil
1 tbsp tomato paste
5fl oz (150ml) red wine
1 bay leaf
2 sprigs of rosemary
4 sprigs of thyme
9oz (250g) shallots
4 carrots
4 parsnips

1. Season the lamb shanks with salt and pepper. Heat 2 tablespoons of oil in a large pot and brown the shanks on all sides, then remove them from the pot. Add the tomato paste to the pot and cook briefly. Pour in the red wine to deglaze the pot and add 3 cups of water. Add the bay leaf, rosemary, and thyme, and bring everything to a boil. Now return the lamb shanks to the pot and season with salt and pepper. Let simmer over low heat for about 1 hour.

2. While the lamb shanks are simmering, peel the shallots, leaving them whole. Cut the carrots and parsnips into thick slices.

3. Heat the remaining oil in a large pan. Add the vegetables and sauté them for about 5 minutes. About 15 minutes before the end of the cooking time, add the root vegetables to the lamb shanks and cook until tender. To deglaze the pan in which you sautéed the vegetables, add a scant ½ cup of water and bring to a boil. Add the liquid to the lamb shanks.

4. Serve the lamb shanks with the root vegetables and the sauce. Dumplings (see p. 104) are good with this, or a simple bread roll.

Two turbulent weeks: Oktoberfest highlights

The celebration of the Theresienwiese typically lasts 16 days. It begins the first Saturday after September 15 and ends the first Sunday in October. If the last Sunday of the fair falls on October 1 or 2, the fair is extended to October 3—German Unity Day—and then lasts 17 or 18 days. Most visitors attend the fair on the three weekends, because not everyone can, or wants to, take time off work during the week to go. However, this isn't such a such a bad idea, taking into account the huge throngs of people on the weekends, and the tents closing due to overcrowding.

Formerly, teams of draft horses were responsible for delivering the beer during the festival. Even today, the splendidly decorated beer wagons pulled by teams of powerful drays plod their way daily to the beer tents, much to the pleasure of fairgoers. However, the beer is usually stored in steel containers—or it arrives, as it does in the Hacker tent, by way of a circular underground "beer pipeline." Only in the Augustiner tents is the golden nectar drawn from large wooden barrels, just as in the olden days.

The Grand Entry

The two-week festival is ushered in with a spectacle both tourists and Munich residents enjoy watching: the Grand Entry of the Oktoberfest Landlords and Breweries. Starting on Saturday morning, the streets of the parade route are closed to traffic. Beginning at 11 am, brewery wagons festively decorated with flowers and bunting, and pulled by teams of dray horses, wind their way through the city center. Passing by the crowds lining the route, they parade from Josephspitalstraße along Sonnenstraße and Schwanthalerstraße, ending at the Theresienwiese. At the head of the parade, on horseback, rides the city's symbol, the Münchner Kindl, dressed in a black-and-yellow monk's habit. Next comes the mayor's carriage, followed by the tent landlords (managers) and their staff. To the sound of jingling harness bells and brass bands, waving to the crowd and often already swinging beer mugs, they accompany flower-bedecked wooden beer kegs to the fairgrounds.

"O'zapft is!"

After the parade ends, a wooden keg takes its place at center stage. At exactly noon, in the Schottenhamel tent, surrounded by celebrities and members of the press, Munich's mayor taps the first keg of Oktoberfest beer. The cry *"O'zapft is!"* ("The barrel is tapped!") officially opens the Oktoberfest. The number of blows it takes the mayor to tap the barrel is always the subject of much speculation and critical scrutiny: the fewer blows, the more in command the mayor appears. This is why the heads of City Hall are more than happy to get a little training from a keg-tapping expert. By tradition, the first beer goes to the Bavarian state premier. Since this is a matter of honor, a blind eye is turned to political differences on this occasion.

Folk costumes and riflemen

The following day, the first Sunday of the Oktoberfest, tradition is king, as this is when the huge Costume and Riflemen's Procession heads to the Theresienwiese.

Thousands cheer as folk groups and rifleman's groups, brass bands, marching bands, and standard bearers march through the city. Among them trundle highly polished coaches and horse-drawn brewery wagons. The parade starts at the Maximilian II monument on the Isar river, progresses along Maximilianstraße through the city center, and finishes at Esperantoplatz in front of the fairgrounds. Finally, the 9,000 parade participants proudly present often highly elaborate, original folk costumes from their regions of origin. They come not just from Bavaria but from all over Germany, other parts of Europe, and even North America. There are also historical costumes on show, from the Middle Ages to Art Nouveau, interspersed with riflemen's and crossbow groups, and men-at-arms. Historic figures such as the mythical Schmied von Kochel or the sculptor Erasmus Grasser are brought to life. The parade is a long-standing tradition: First held in 1835 on the occasion of the silver wedding anniversary of Ludwig I and Therese von Bayern, it has been staged at every Oktoberfest since 1948. Many visitors consider it to be the most integral part of the Oktoberfest.

Visitors from the South

A different kind of party starts on the second weekend of the fair. Thousands of Italians come to Munich that weekend for the "festival della birra" (festival of beer). At 19 percent, Italians are the largest group of Oktoberfest visitors, and the party atmosphere sizzles during the so-called Italian weekend.

On the final evening of the festival, it's unavoidable: The waiters serve the last mugs of beer. Emotional closing ceremonies are held in each tent. Sparklers and sing-alongs transform the tents into something very special indeed during the final minutes of the fair. Quite a few visitors and waiting staff have tears of farewell running down their cheeks. But there is one consolation: With the ending of this year's Oktoberfest, you can start looking forward to next year's festival!

Crispy duck
with apple and onion stuffing

On the fairgrounds, ducks are roasted on the spit like chickens. At home, in the meantime, it's better to roast the duck slowly in the oven—that way, you get a lovely gravy, too.

Serves 4–6 · Prep time: 25 minutes · Cooking time: 2 hours

1 duck, about 5½lb (2.5kg)
salt, pepper
2 apples
4 onions
1 tsp dried marjoram
¼ cup chopped celery root
¼ cup chopped carrot
1 cup chopped leek
⅔ cup chopped parsnip
4 sprigs of flat-leaf parsley
4 sprigs of mugwort (optional)

1. Preheat the oven to 350°F (180°C). Pat the duck dry, then season inside and out with salt and pepper.

2. To make the filling, wash the apples, then quarter and core them. Peel 2 of the onions. Coarsely chop both the apples and onions, mix together, and season with marjoram, salt, and pepper. Stuff the duck with the apple-and-onion mixture and place it in a roasting pan.

3. Add about 1 cup of water to the roasting pan and roast the duck in the middle of the preheated oven for about 2 hours. Baste the duck occasionally with the juices. Add a little water as required. If the skin turns too dark or does not brown enough, reduce or increase the oven temperature.

4. While the duck cooks, peel the remaining onions and coarsely chop. After 1 hour of the cooking time, scatter the onions, chopped vegetables, and the parsley and mugwort sprigs, if using, around the duck in the roasting pan.

5. At the end of the cooking time, remove the duck from the roasting pan and keep warm. Pour the sauce through a fine mesh sieve into a second pot and set aside for a few minutes. Then carefully skim off the fat that has risen to the surface and return the sauce to a boil.

6. Carve the duck into four to six portions and remove the filling. Serve with the filling, the sauce, dumplings (see p. 104), and red cabbage (see p. 99).

Bavarian chicken hash
with fresh vegetables

Believe it or not, sometimes there is actually a roasted Oktoberfest chicken left over—and it is perfect for this very fine hash.

Serves 4 · Prep time: 40 minutes · Cooling time: 1 hour

1¾lb (800g) yellow potatoes, such as Yukon Gold (or boiled potatoes left over from the day before)
salt
1lb 2oz (500g) mixed vegetables (such as green beans, cauliflower, carrots)
2 onions
1 roasted chicken (see p. 74)
2 tbsp vegetable oil
pepper
2 tbsp chopped parsley, to garnish

1. Boil the potatoes in salted water for about 20 minutes, or until cooked. Drain, let the steam evaporate briefly, and peel. Leave the potatoes to cool for about 1 hour, then cut them into slices.

2. In a second pot, bring salted water to a boil. Add the green beans and blanch them until they are tender but still firm. Plunge into ice water and drain in a sieve. Cut the cauliflower into small florets and slice the carrots. Peel the onions and slice into rings.

3. Remove the chicken meat from the bone and cut it into bite-size pieces. Heat the oil in one large or two small pans. Add the potatoes, green beans, cauliflower, carrots, onions, and chicken pieces. Stirring often, cook the chicken and vegetables over high heat for about 10 minutes until golden brown.

4. Season the hash with salt and pepper, sprinkle with chopped parsley, and serve immediately.

Tip: Hash, or "Gröstl," is a classic Bavarian recipe for using up leftovers. To make it, use anything you like or whatever you happen to have in the refrigerator. The chicken can be substituted with roast pork, roast duck, cooked beef, smoked bacon, or ham. And instead of boiled potatoes, try potato dumplings, bread dumplings, or pretzel dumplings. Select the fresh vegetables that are in season: leek, broccoli, bell pepper, and celery also work well in this hash. Or leave out the vegetables entirely. If you feel like it, serve fried eggs with the hash, or whisk 2 or 3 eggs, pour them over the hash toward the end of the cooking time, and leave to set.

Oktoberfest chicken

Eating chicken with your fingers is absolutely allowed at the Oktoberfest—because, after all, things are a bit more rustic here, and the roasted chicken is easier to pull apart without cutlery.

Serves 4 · Prep time: 15 minutes · Cooking time: 45 minutes

1 tbsp paprika
1 pinch of cayenne pepper
1 tsp curry powder
1 tsp sugar
salt, pepper
2 roasting chickens (2lb/900g each)
4 sprigs of flat-leaf parsley
2 tbsp unsalted butter

You will also need
salt for the baking tray

1. Place an oven rack in the middle of the oven, then preheat the oven to 350°F (180°C). Sprinkle a layer of salt about ½in (1cm) thick on a baking or roasting tray. Place the tray on the next oven rack down. Alternatively, fire up the grill and prepare the rotisserie.

2. Combine the paprika, cayenne pepper, curry powder, sugar, salt, and pepper in a small bowl. Pat the chickens dry. Then rub the seasoning into the chickens, inside and out. Put 2 sprigs of parsley and 1 tablespoon of butter in each cavity.

3. Place the chickens directly on the oven rack above the salted tray. Roast the chickens for about 45 minutes, or until they are fully cooked and the skin is nice and crisp. Alternatively, skewer the chickens on the rotisserie and grill them until cooked.

4. Cut the chickens in half lengthwise and then into servings. Serve with potato salad (see p. 110), pretzel snails and chestnuts (see p. 113), or pretzels.

Tip: To make roast ham hocks, or "Schweinshaxn," combine 1 teaspoon each of caraway seeds and paprika with salt and pepper. Use the spice mix to liberally season 4 fresh (not smoked or pickled) ham hocks—ask the butcher to score the skin for you. Roast or grill the hocks as described above for 90 minutes. About 30 minutes before they are done, baste the hocks with 1 cup of Oktoberfest beer. Serve with Bavarian cabbage (see p. 99) or Bavarian cabbage slaw (see p. 100).

Pan-fried char
with lemon-and-parsley butter

Fish dredged in flour and pan-fried with just a few simple ingredients—butter, lemon, and parsley—is the Bavarians' favorite way of preparing the abundant freshwater fish of the region.

Serves 4 · Prep time: 30 minutes

4 whole char, about ¾lb (350g) each
salt, pepper
all-purpose flour, for dredging
oil, for frying
¼ cup unsalted butter
2 tbsp chopped parsley
juice of 1 lemon
lemon wedges, to serve

1. Rinse the char in cold water, pat them dry, and season inside and out with salt and pepper. Sprinkle flour on a large plate. Dredge the fish on both sides in the flour and shake off the excess.

2. Heat some oil in two large pans. Place 2 char in each pan, reduce the heat, and fry the fish on each side for about 5 minutes, basting them frequently with the hot oil.

3. Carefully drain off the oil. Melt the butter in the frying pans and continue frying the fish, gently shaking the pans back and forth to make the butter foam. Add the chopped parsley and lemon juice, and shake the pans again.

4. Lift the fish out of the frying pans and serve immediately, garnished with lemon wedges and accompanied by parslied potatoes (see p. 103).

Tip: To make original "Steckerlfisch"—fish grilled on a stick—you need whole fish spitted on sticks and the outdoor grill specially designed to cook the fish on, or embers with sand piled all around, just like it's done at the fair. However, fish cooked on a charcoal grill in your backyard tastes just as good. Use 1 whole cleaned and washed fish (such as char, trout, or mackerel) per person, season liberally with salt and pepper, and put 1 sprig of thyme in each cavity. Cook the fish on the hot grill for about 5 minutes on each side, or until done.

Beer battered fish
with remoulade sauce

In predominantly Catholic Bavaria, it is customary to eat fish on Fridays. Tradition and church are closely linked here; children are even baptized at the fair during the annual ecumenical service that is always held in one of the gigantic beer tents.

Serves 4 · Prep time: 50 minutes

For the remoulade sauce
2 dill pickles (from the jar), finely chopped
1 tbsp capers (from the jar), finely chopped
2 anchovy fillets, finely chopped
¼ cup mayonnaise
5½oz (150g) plain yogurt
2 tbsp chopped parsley
salt, pepper

For the battered fish
4 fish fillets for deep-frying (such as cod, hake, haddock, or pollock)
juice of 1 lemon
salt, pepper
1¼ cups all-purpose flour
5fl oz (150ml) Oktoberfest beer
2 large eggs
oil, for deep frying
lemon wedges, to serve

1. Make the remoulade sauce: in a bowl, stir together the dill pickles, capers, anchovies, mayonnaise, yogurt, and parsley. Season with salt and pepper and chill until serving time.

2. To prepare the fish, rinse the fillets with cold water and pat dry. Drizzle with the lemon juice and season with salt and pepper.

3. Whisk the flour and beer together to make a thick batter, and season it with salt and pepper. Separate the eggs and stir the egg yolks into the batter. In a separate bowl, beat the egg whites until they form stiff peaks. Carefully fold the beaten egg whites into the batter.

4. Heat enough oil in a shallow pan for the fish to float when you fry them. One at a time, dip the fish fillets into the batter, allow any excess to drip off, and immediately lower the fish into the hot oil. Fry on each side for about 5 minutes until golden brown. Using a slotted spoon, lift the fillets out of the oil and let drain on paper towels.

5. Cut the remaining lemon into wedges. Serve the fish immediately, with the remoulade sauce and the lemon wedges on the side. Potato salad (see p. 110) goes well with this.

Vegetarian & side dishes

Spinach spaetzle
with fried onions

Spinach spaetzle and cheese spaetzle are particularly popular with fair visitors from the United States. Perhaps this Swabian-Bavarian classic with its layers of melted cheese reminds them of classic American macaroni and cheese.

Serves 4 · Prep time: 40 minutes

1lb (450g) chopped frozen spinach
salt
2 cups all-purpose flour
¾ cup semolina
3 eggs
pepper
1 pinch of grated nutmeg
5½oz (150g) freshly grated Swiss cheese
2 onions, peeled and sliced into rings
1 tbsp unsalted butter, plus more for the casserole dish

You will also need
a spaetzle maker

1. Defrost the spinach according to the instructions on the package. Preheat the oven to 350°F (180°C). Butter an ovenproof dish.

2. In a large pot, bring a generous amount of salted water to a boil. In a large bowl, combine the flour and semolina. Add the eggs and spinach, and season with salt, pepper, and nutmeg. Beat the mixture to make a thick batter that drips slowly off a wooden spoon. Continue beating vigorously for about 5 minutes, until small bubbles form.

3. Ladle a portion of batter into the spaetzle maker and grate the spaetzle straight into the boiling water. When the spaetzle float to the surface, remove them with a slotted spoon and drain briefly. Place a layer of spinach spaetzle in the casserole dish and top with a layer of grated cheese, then put the dish in the oven to keep warm. Continue in this way until the dough and cheese are all used up.

4. Melt the butter in a pan and sauté the onions until golden brown. Top the spaetzle with the fried onions and serve immediately. A leafy green salad goes well with this dish.

Tip: For classic spaetzle, combine 2 cups all-purpose flour, ¾ cup semolina, 4 eggs, salt, grated nutmeg, and 1 cup of cold water to make a batter, and cook as described above. To serve, cut 2 tablespoons of unsalted butter into small pieces and stir into the spaetzle. They make an excellent side dish for sauerbraten (see p. 58) and venison stew (see p. 65), for example.

Vegetarian & side dishes

Sauerkraut strudel

You can roll up many different kinds of fillings in strudel dough. Sweet things are usually hidden inside—not, however, in this savory version made with sauerkraut. Sauerkraut strudel tastes equally good fresh from the oven or sliced and served cold as part of an Oktoberfest party buffet.

Makes 12 pieces · Prep time: 1 hour · Resting time: 30 minutes · Baking time: 45 minutes

For the dough
2 cups all-purpose flour, plus more for the work surface
salt
1 egg
2 tbsp vegetable oil
3 tbsp unsalted butter
2 handfuls of breadcrumbs

For the filling
1 recipe sauerkraut (see p. 44)

1 To make the dough, sift together the flour and salt. Add the egg, oil, and about ⅔ cup of lukewarm water. Using your hands, knead the mixture to make a moderately firm dough. Rinse a bowl with warm water, invert it over the dough, and leave to rest at room temperature for about 30 minutes.

2 For the filling, prepare the sauerkraut (see p. 44) and set aside to cool, then put it in a sieve to drain.

3 Preheat the oven to 350°F (180°C). Line a baking tray with parchment paper. Place the dough on the floured work surface and knead vigorously, then roll out thinly. Dust a clean dish towel with flour and place the rolled-out dough on top. Using your hands, stretch the dough as thinly as possible to form a rectangle about 16×24in (40x60cm) in size.

4 Melt the butter and brush on to the sheet of dough. Reserve the remaining butter. Scatter the breadcrumbs over the dough, then spread the sauerkraut evenly over the breadcrumbs. Leave a clear edge about 1in (3cm) wide so the sauerkraut does not squeeze out of the sides when you roll up the strudel. Using the dish towel, and working from the long end, roll up the dough to form a strudel. Place the strudel on the baking tray, seam side down, and tuck the ends underneath. Brush the top with the remaining melted butter and bake the strudel in the middle of the preheated oven for about 45 minutes.

5 Remove the strudel from the oven, cut into twelve pieces, and serve. A mixed salad or pork sausages go well with this dish.

Tip: If you like, you can roll up 6 grilled pork sausages or vegetarian sausages into the strudel, along with the sauerkraut.

Potato chip spirals
with two kinds of dips

You will need a little patience to cut the potatoes into spirals, but it's worth the effort! Fresh from the deep-fryer, they are deliciously crisp and taste just as good when made at home as when eaten while sauntering over the fairgrounds.

Serves 4 · Prep time: 35 minutes

For the herb dip
1 squeeze of fresh lemon juice
2 tbsp chopped herbs (such as dill, parsley, and chives)
7oz (200g) Greek yogurt (not non-fat)
salt, pepper

For the chili dip
1 tsp smoked hot paprika
½ tsp chili flakes
½ tsp dried thyme
¾ cup ketchup

For the potato spirals
8 large yellow potatoes, such as Yukon Gold
oil, for deep frying
salt

You will also need
a spiralizer or a spiral radish cutter

1. To make the herb dip, stir the lemon juice and chopped herbs into the yogurt. Season with salt and pepper. Refrigerate until ready to serve.

2. To make the chili dip, stir the paprika, chili flakes, and thyme into the ketchup. As with the herb dip, refrigerate until ready to serve.

3. To make the potato spirals, use a spiralizer or a spiral radish cutter to cut the potatoes into long spirals. Pat the spirals dry with a dish towel.

4. In a shallow pan, heat a generous amount of oil for deep-frying the potatoes. Working in batches, put the potato spirals into the hot oil, and as you do so, stretch them out a little. Fry the spirals for about 5 minutes until they are crisp, turning them frequently and keeping them loose. Using a slotted spoon, lift the spirals out of the oil onto paper towels to drain.

5. Sprinkle the hot potato spirals with salt or seasoning (see tip). Serve immediately, with the chilled dips on the side.

Tip: This easy seasoning mix gives the freshly fried potato spirals an extra kick: stir together 1 teaspoon of sugar, 1 tablespoon of paprika, ½ teaspoon of ground caraway seeds, and 1 pinch each of cayenne pepper and salt.

Creamy wild mushroom stew

The Bavarians lovingly call mushrooms "Schwammerl" and enjoy them most when they are cooked in a creamy sauce. This mushroom stew is particularly delicious when prepared with the fresh chanterelle and porcini mushrooms that are in season in the woods during the Oktoberfest.

Serves 4 · Prep time: 1 hour

1 onion
1lb 2oz (500g) mixed mushrooms (such as chanterelles, porcini, cremini, or white mushrooms)
clarified unsalted butter, for frying
3½fl oz (100ml) white wine
salt, pepper
1¾ cups heavy cream
2 tbsp chopped parsley

1 Prepare the vegetables: peel the onion and dice it finely. Cut the mushrooms in half or slice them, depending on their size.

2 Heat a little clarified butter in a large pan. Add the onion and mushrooms and sauté over high heat for about 5 minutes. Add the white wine to deglaze the pan and cook until the wine has completely evaporated. Only then, season the mushrooms with salt and pepper. Pour in the cream and boil for about 5 minutes, or until the sauce has thickened slightly.

3 Ladle the mushroom stew into bowls, sprinkle with chopped parsley, and serve. Bread dumplings (see p. 104) are the perfect accompaniment.

Tip: Creamy wild mushroom stew also makes a great sauce to accompany pan-fried cuts of meat such as pork tenderloin medallions, rump steak, schnitzel, or strips of veal. To cook, first fry the meat of your choice, remove from the pan, and keep warm. Using the same pan, prepare the mushroom stew as described above and serve with the meat. The stew is also perfect with classic spaetzle (see tip p. 82).

Oktoberfest attractions: Hang on tight and don't let go!

The Oktoberfest has a truly overwhelming abundance of attractions and rides. But where to start, where to stop, and what is absolutely unmissable? Many of the fair's approximately 200 concessions have a long tradition; some have been around since the beginning of the 20th century. The more nostalgic rides are particularly popular, both with locals and tourists. Often these rides have been in family hands for as many as three or four generations.

Cult rides

"Auf geht's beim Schichtl!" ("Let the Schichtl show begin!") Many have followed this call over the years, and it has become a familiar saying in Bavaria. Since 1869, heads have rolled in this "original magic specialty theater" show created by Michael August Schichtl. The short performances feature all manner of curiosities. You can watch the "beheading of a living person by means of the guillotine," or put yourself forward as a candidate for the same treatment. If that's not your thing, you could dress up at the Royal Bavarian Court Photographer and have your "vintage" photograph taken in period style, or be astonished by the mini-athletes in the Flohzirkus (flea circus). The action is wilder at "Pitts Todeswand" (Pitt's death wall), where motorcycle and go-cart daredevils have shown off their driving skills since 1928.

One fun and decidedly "cult" ride at the fair is the Teufelsrad (Devil's Wheel), which has been entertaining fairgoers since 1910. The devilish part is the circular rotating platform, approximately 16ft (5m) across, on which the riders sit. The longer it rotates, the harder it is for those on the platform to resist the centrifugal force and not slide off. The riders who hold on the longest are eventually swept off by ropes and large foam balls. But the best part is the running commentary, delivered with earthy Bavarian humor by the "Rekommandeur" at the expense of the guests.

Schadenfreude—delight in the misfortune of others—is also in play on the Toboggan. This ride has been an attraction at the fair since 1908 and is now no longer set up anywhere else. This wooden slide is in itself harmless, but to get to the top requires a ride on a mean and very fast-moving conveyor belt. If you've had a few beers, it can definitely put a dent in your performance! People flail helplessly trying to hold on to the railing that doesn't actually move with the conveyor belt, leading them to travel to the top feet- or bottom-first.

Perhaps it's best to avoid disgrace, and climb aboard the Krinoline instead. Moving gently up and down as it revolves to the comfortable tempo of a live brass band, this old-fashioned carousel has been an Oktoberfest attraction since 1924. Its name is a reference to the bouncing hooped skirts worn by women in the second half of the 19th century. At first, the Munich Krinoline was operated solely by muscle power, but in 1937 it was electrified. Not too long afterward, Michael Großmann, the concession owner at the time, had a brilliant idea: He hired a brass band. Since then, the ride has been accompanied by Bavarian mood music.

Hi-tech tests of courage

For high-end thrill seekers with cast-iron stomachs, the fair offers an enormous number of modern rides, each of them promising a huge adrenaline rush. "Higher,

further, faster," as they say, and there's a new attraction every year. Cyber Space, Top Spin, High Energy, and Frisbee are the names of these dizzying thrill rides that take you up, down, to the right, to the left, and upside down. They are certainly not for everyone.

There are nostalgic rides, too. Some of these take you "Rund um the Tegernsee" ("around Lake Tegernsee"), or around a winter landscape complete with snowman on the Zugspitzbahn. You can't be afraid of heights if you decide to ride up the Skyfall-Turm or the Power Tower II to platforms 265ft (80m) high, only to plunge to Earth at a terrifying speed. For a similar effect on your stomach, try one of the many other roller coasters. Among them is the Olympia-Looping, supposedly the largest traveling roller coaster in the world. It has five loops and reaches a speed of more than 60 miles (100km) per hour. It has had a permanent slot on the fairgrounds since 1989. Another institution is the very popular Alpinabahn, which does not turn riders upside down but hurtles downhill at breathtaking speed.

High up in the air

Rather than plummeting earthward, some might prefer gliding through the air instead. So it's off to a ride on the good old Kettenkarussell, the swing ride!

The Kalb family set up their first swing ride on the Theresienwiese in 1919. It was replaced in 2004 by the more modern wave swinger, Circus Welt. The soft clinking of the steel chains when the seats bump into one another, the wind in your hair, and the candied almonds you can nibble on during a flight make this a favorite for many visitors to the fairgrounds—apart from all the other classics, of course, such as the bumper cars and the swinging ship. Last but not least there's the big Ferris wheel, an absolute must. When you are 164ft (50m) up in the air, the gondolas—decorated with hearts and blue-and-white checks—offer a sensational view of the Theresienwiese and Munich. Go after dark to see the beautiful lights.

There also are many attractions for the youngest fans of the fair, from the blue-and-white Münchner Rutsch'n with its wavy slides, to the many children's carousels, to the Wilde Maus (Wild Mouse). The latter has a very particular way of going around the curves, which is a lot of fun for adults, too. For horror fans of all ages, the "Geisterbahn," or haunted house, is the place to go: The bravest choose one featuring live ghosts. The Irrgarten, or fun house, can be a challenge even for adult visitors. You can also try your luck at one of the many shooting stands and other carnival games. You'll be popular with the little ones if you can win a stuffed toy at one of these.

The Old Fair

Since 2010, the Oktoberfest has been enriched by another popular attraction, perhaps *the* most popular: the "Oide Wiesn," or Old Fair. This amusement park, with its rides and beer tents that take you back to the old days of the Oktoberfest, was set up in the south section of the Theresienwiese in 2010 to mark the 200th anniversary of the Oktoberfest. It was so well received that it was made a permanent part of the Oktoberfest. Every four years it has to make way for the Bavarian Agricultural Fair, which takes place on the same spot.

The Old Fair is different: It is not the rowdy festival where everything is bigger and better, or a wild party. Here things are slower and gentler, traditionally Bavarian and with a great atmosphere. In the two popular tents, Tradition and Herzkasperl, beer is served in pottery mugs, or steins, as in the past. And people don't dance on the benches, but on the dedicated dance floor or in front of the stage. Bands come from all over Bavaria to perform here. The Herzkasperl tent offers a platform for younger artists, some of whom are from the regional music scene. In the Tradition tent, great brass bands, folk dance groups, and whip-crackers provide the atmosphere. Another attraction is the "Humoristische Velodrom"; the fun bike races held here require equal amounts of speed and dexterity. In front of the tent, old-fashioned rides, ring tossing, and similar pleasures vie for the attention of the public.

Here you will also find the original Kalb swing ride dating back to 1919, and a ride on the vintage Calypso, with its colorful, decorated gondolas, will make you feel like you have traveled back in time. With its marionette theater, pony run, swinging ship, old-fashioned carousel, and varied entertainment, the Old Fair has a great deal to offer, especially for children and families. For a modest entrance fee of 3 Euro, you can remain on the grounds of the traditional fair all day, from 10am to 10pm. The rides themselves usually cost 1 Euro each, so all in all, this is relatively affordable fun. Concessions stop serving alcohol at around 9:30pm, an hour earlier than on the main fairgrounds. This might seem a little early, but it has one definite advantage: You go to bed earlier and are fit enough the next day to return and continue the celebration.

Grünkern (spelt) patties with paprika

The Oktoberfest follows trends, too, and year after year you will find more vegetarian and vegan treats here, such as these patties made with grünkern. Grünkern—unripe spelt—has always been a popular ingredient for vegetarian dishes in Bavarian cuisine.

Serves 4 · Prep time: 50 minutes

oil, for frying
1½ cups medium whole grünkern groats (unripe spelt grains)
2 cups vegetable broth
1 onion
1 red bell pepper
3 sprigs of thyme
salt, pepper
2 large eggs
3½oz (100g) grated Swiss cheese
2–3 tbsp breadcrumbs
1 tbsp paprika

1. Heat 1 tablespoon of oil in a pot and sauté the grünkern until light brown. Pour in the vegetable broth and simmer the grains over low heat, stirring constantly, for about 5 minutes. Remove the pot from the heat and leave the grünkern to swell for about 20 minutes, then set aside to cool.

2. Meanwhile, peel the onion and remove the stem and seeds from the bell pepper. Finely dice the onion and pepper. In a pan, heat 1 tablespoon of oil, add the onion, and sauté. Then add the diced pepper and thyme, and sauté with the onion. Season with salt and pepper and remove the thyme sprigs.

3. In a large bowl, combine the cooked grünkern with the pepper and onion mixture, the eggs, cheese, and the breadcrumbs, until you have a mixture that is easy to shape. Season with salt, pepper, and paprika, then moisten your hands and make 8 patties from the spelt mixture.

4. Heat a little oil in a large pan, add the spelt patties, and fry them on each side for about 10 minutes. Remove from the pan and serve with carrot and cabbage salad (see p. 100). If you like, serve a dip alongside (see p. 86).

Creamy Savoy cabbage with fried eggs

...or "ox eyes," as fried eggs are often called in Bavaria. The fried eggs turn the creamy cabbage into a main dish; without them, it also makes a great side for many meat dishes.

Serves 4 · Prep time: 45 minutes

- 1 small head of Savoy cabbage (about 1lb 5oz/600g), cut into square pieces about ¾×¾in (2×2cm) in size
- salt
- 2 carrots, sliced
- unsalted butter for frying
- 1 onion, peeled and finely diced
- 1 tbsp all-purpose flour
- 1¾ cups vegetable broth
- 1 cup heavy cream
- pepper
- grated nutmeg
- 1 tsp caraway seeds
- 4–8 eggs
- paprika, to serve

1 In a large pot, bring salted water to a boil. Blanch the cabbage pieces first, until tender but firm to the bite. Repeat with the sliced carrots. Drain the cabbage and carrots in a sieve, plunge them into ice water, and drain again.

2 Melt 1 tablespoon of butter in a pot, add the diced onion, and sauté. Dust the onion with flour and pour in the vegetable broth. Stirring constantly, boil the sauce for about 10 minutes. Stir in the cream.

3 Add the Savoy cabbage and carrots to the sauce. Season the vegetables with salt, pepper, nutmeg, and caraway seeds, and cook for about 5 minutes.

4 Heat a little butter in a large frying pan (you may have to do this in two portions, or two frying pans). Break the eggs gently into the pans and fry them over a low heat for about 5 minutes until the whites have set.

5 Portion out the creamy cabbage onto plates, top each with a fried egg or two, and sprinkle with paprika, to taste. Serve with salt and pepper, for the eggs, and parslied potatoes (see p. 103).

Tip: Creamy Savoy cabbage pairs well as a side for beef roulades (see p. 61), venison stew (see p. 65), or stuffed breast of veal (see p. 54).

Vegetarian & side dishes

Red cabbage

Serves 4 · Prep time: 25 minutes · Cooking time: 50 minutes

- 1 onion, peeled, sliced into rings
- 2 apples, quartered, cored, and thinly sliced
- 1 small head of red cabbage, about 1¾lb (800g), sliced into thin strips
- 2 tbsp vegetable oil
- 7fl oz (200ml) red wine
- 2 cups vegetable broth
- salt
- ½ tsp black peppercorns
- 1 clove
- 1 bay leaf
- 1 tbsp cornstarch
- 2 tbsp cooked cranberries, lingonberries, or fresh red currants

1. Heat the oil in a large pot. Add the onion and apples, and sauté. Add the cabbage and sauté it briefly. Pour in the red wine to deglaze the pot and boil until it has completely evaporated. Pour in the vegetable broth, season with salt, peppercorns, clove, and bay leaf, and simmer over low heat for about 45 minutes, stirring now and then.

2. Stir 2 tablespoons of cold water into the cornstarch. Stir the cornstarch mixture into the cabbage and boil for about 5 minutes.

3. Just before serving, fold the cooked cranberries, lingonberries, or fresh red currants into the cabbage. Red cabbage goes well with dishes such as crispy duck (see p. 70), venison stew (see p. 65) or sauerbraten (see p. 58).

Bavarian cabbage

Serves 4 · Prep time: 20 minutes · Cooking time: 45 minutes

- 1 onion, peeled and sliced into rings
- 2 tbsp vegetable oil
- 1 small head of white cabbage (about 1¾lb/800g), cut into square pieces about ¾×¾in (2×2cm) in size
- 1 tsp sugar
- 1 tsp caraway seeds
- 2 cups vegetable broth
- salt
- 1 tbsp white wine vinegar

1. Heat the oil in a large pot, add the onion, and sauté. Sprinkle the sugar over the onions and cook them until golden brown and lightly caramelized.

2. Add the cabbage and caraway seeds and cook briefly. Then pour in the vegetable broth and simmer the cabbage over low heat for about 45 minutes, stirring now and then. Season with salt.

3. Just before serving, stir in the white wine vinegar. Bavarian cabbage is a great accompaniment for dishes such as roast suckling pig (see p. 47), roast ham hocks (see tip p. 74), or boiled ham hocks (see p. 44), instead of sauerkraut.

Bavarian cabbage slaw

Serves 4 · Prep time: 25 minutes

1 small head of white cabbage (about 1¾lb/800g), cut into very thin strips
salt
¼ cup white wine vinegar
¼ cup vegetable oil
pepper
1 tsp caraway seeds

1 Put the cabbage strips into a bowl and salt generously. Using your hands, vigorously knead the cabbage for about 5 minutes until it has significantly softened and become glassy.

2 Add the vinegar and oil to the cabbage and toss. Season the salad with pepper and caraway seeds, and leave it to marinate for about 15 minutes. The slaw goes very well with dishes such as roast ham hocks (see tip p. 74), roast suckling pig (see p. 47), or stuffed breast of veal (see p. 54).

Tip: *For some extra crunch, cut 5½oz (150g) of well marbled smoked bacon or smoked tofu into small cubes. Heat 1 tablespoon of oil in a pan, add the bacon or tofu, and cook until crisp. Add the cooked bacon or tofu to the slaw, toss, and marinate as described above, but use only 3 tablespoons of vegetable oil for the marinade.*

Carrot and cabbage slaw

Serves 4 · Prep time: 25 minutes

½ head of white cabbage (about 14oz/400g), cut into very thin strips
salt
4 carrots, grated
¼ cup apple cider vinegar
¼ cup vegetable oil
pepper
1 tsp sugar
2 tbsp chopped parsley

1 Put the cabbage strips into a bowl and salt generously. Using your hands, vigorously knead the cabbage for about 5 minutes until it has significantly softened and become glassy.

2 Add the grated carrots to the cabbage. Stir in the vinegar and oil, and toss well. Season with pepper, to taste, add the sugar, toss well, and leave to marinate for about 15 minutes.

3 Just before serving, sprinkle chopped parsley over the slaw. Carrot and cabbage slaw is good with dishes such as pork schnitzel cordon bleu (see p. 43) or spelt patties (see p. 94).

Tip: *If you like your salad a little fruity, grate 1 apple and add it to the cabbage along with the carrots.*

Parslied potatoes

Serves 4 · Prep time: 30 minutes

1¾lb (800g) yellow potatoes, such as Yukon Gold
salt
2 tbsp unsalted butter
2 tbsp chopped parsley

1 Peel and wash the potatoes. Depending on their size, cut them into halves or quarters. Boil the potatoes in salted water for about 20 minutes, or until cooked, then drain.

2 Melt the butter in a large pan and heat until it foams. Add the potatoes and chopped parsley, and shake the pan back and forth until the potatoes are coated on all sides with the parsley butter. Parslied potatoes go very well with dishes such as boiled beef (see p. 57), boiled ham hocks (see p. 44), or pan-fried char (see p. 77).

Classic mashed potatoes

Serves 4 · Prep time: 30 minutes

2¼lb (1kg) white potatoes, such as Russet potatoes
salt
1 cup milk
2 tbsp unsalted butter
1 pinch of grated nutmeg

1 Peel and wash the potatoes. Depending on their size, cut them into halves or quarters. Boil in salted water for about 20 minutes, or until cooked. Drain the potatoes and mash well with a potato masher.

2 Boil the milk. Stir the butter into the potatoes. Then pour in the hot milk and stir. Finally, season the mashed potatoes with freshly grated nutmeg. Classic mashed potatoes go well with sauce-rich dishes such as beef roulades (see p. 61), sauerbraten (see p. 58), boiled ham hocks on a bed of sauerkraut (see p. 44), or just on their own, topped with fried onions.

Vegetarian & side dishes

Dumpling essentials

Potato dumplings

Serves 4 · Prep time: 1 hour

3⅓lb (1.5kg) white potatoes, such as Russet potatoes
salt
¼ cup potato starch
½ day-old bread roll
1 tbsp unsalted butter

1 Peel and wash half the potatoes. Depending on size, cut them into halves or quarters. Boil them in salted water for about 20 minutes, or until done, and drain. Return them to the pot for about 5 minutes to let the steam evaporate, then put them through a potato ricer, or mash thoroughly with a potato masher.

2 Peel, wash, and finely grate the remaining potatoes. Put the grated potato on a clean dish towel and twist together. Working over a bowl, squeeze out the liquid from the potatoes and set aside for five minutes, until the starch separates. Carefully pour away the liquid, leaving the potato starch behind. Combine the boiled and raw potatoes and the potato starch from the bowl. Season the mixture with salt to taste.

3 Cut the bread roll into small cubes. Melt the butter in a pan, add the bread, and fry until golden brown. Remove the cubes from the pan.

4 Boil salted water in a large pot. Shape peach-size dumplings from the potato mixture, press a few bread cubes into the center of each, and reshape. Drop into the boiling water and simmer over low heat for 20 minutes, or until cooked. Lift the dumplings out of the pot with a slotted spoon and serve. These make a good side for sauce-rich meat dishes, or can be served just with sauce for children.

Bread dumplings

Makes 4 portions · Prep time: 45 minutes

8 day-old bread rolls
1 cup milk
1 tbsp unsalted butter
1 onion, peeled and diced
2 large eggs
2 tbsp chopped flat-leaf parsley
salt, pepper
1 pinch of grated nutmeg

1 Finely slice the bread rolls and put them in a bowl. Boil the milk, pour it over the bread, mix thoroughly, and leave to soak for about 15 minutes.

2 Melt the butter in a pan, add the onion, and sauté. Add the fried onion, eggs, and parsley to the bread-and-milk mixture. Combine thoroughly and season with salt, pepper, and nutmeg.

3 Bring salted water to a boil in a large pot. Shape peach-size dumplings from the bread mixture. Drop the dumplings in the boiling water and simmer over low heat for 20 minutes, or until cooked. Lift the dumplings out of the pot with a slotted spoon and serve with roast suckling pig (see p. 47), sauerbraten (see p. 58), or creamy wild mushroom stew (see p. 89).

Vegetable-stuffed ravioli with fried onions

These ravioli have a delectable vegetable filling. Rolling out the dough and filling the pasta takes some work, but you'll be rewarded with an incomparable treat!

Serves 4 · Prep time: 1 hour

For the pasta
2½ cups flour, plus more for the work surface
⅔ cup semolina
salt
5 eggs
1 tbsp vegetable oil

For the filling
2 day-old bread rolls
2 carrots
¼ celery root
1 leek
1 tbsp unsalted butter
2 tbsp chopped flat-leaf parsley
2 large eggs
1 handful of breadcrumbs
salt, pepper
1 pinch of grated nutmeg

To serve
2 onions, peeled and finely diced
3 tbsp unsalted butter
2 tbsp chopped parsley

You will also need
a pasta maker

1. To make the pasta, combine the flour, semolina, and salt in a bowl. Add 4 eggs and the oil, and knead for about 5 minutes to make a moderately firm dough. Cover in plastic wrap and refrigerate for about 30 minutes.

2. To make the filling, put the bread rolls in a bowl of water and soak for about 30 minutes. Meanwhile, finely dice the carrots, celery root, and leek. Melt the butter in a large pan, add the diced vegetables, and sauté for about 10 minutes. Put the vegetables in a bowl and set aside to cool.

3. Squeeze the soaked bread to remove the excess water, and purée. Combine the bread, diced vegetables, parsley, eggs, and breadcrumbs. Season the mixture with salt, pepper, and nutmeg and set aside until needed.

4. Cut the dough in half. Use a pasta maker to make two very thin sheets of pasta about $\frac{1}{16}$ (1mm) thick. Alternatively, roll out the dough on the floured work surface to make very thin sheets. Place one sheet on the work surface. Drop heaped tablespoonfuls of the vegetable mixture all over the sheet, leaving a large gap between spoonfuls. Whisk the remaining egg and brush it onto the pasta in the gaps between fillings. Place the second sheet of dough on top and press down gently. Cut out squares about ¼×¼in (6×6cm) in size and press the edges together. Place the ravioli side by side on a floured baking tray.

5. Bring a large pot of salted water to a boil. Add the ravioli and simmer over low heat for about 5 minutes, until they are done.

6. In the meantime, peel the onions and dice them finely. Melt 1 tablespoon of the butter in a pan, add the diced onions, and sauté until golden brown. Melt the remaining butter in one large, or two small, pans. Using a slotted spoon, remove the ravioli from the water and drain, then cook them in the hot butter. Sprinkle the pan-fried onions and chopped parsley over the ravioli and serve. A green salad goes well with this dish.

Tip: If you don't have much patience for dicing vegetables, here's a little shortcut: simply grate the carrots and celery root, and slice the leek into very thin rings.

Oktoberfest etiquette

The Oktoberfest may appear unruly, but in fact, following the festival's etiquette is a key part of the fun. Bear in mind these few simple rules and tricks to get the most out of your evening—and to avoid the most unpleasant consequences of overindulgence.

The beer means business

Oktoberfest beer can be perilous due to its higher alcohol content. The most important beer tent rule is simple: Know your limits. Don't drink more than you can handle. A Mass doesn't have to be emptied completely: Leave the dregs (the Bavarians call this the "Noagerl") and order a fresh one. You don't want to spend an evening at the fair nursing stale beer, and clinking glasses is more fun with a fresh Mass. In practically all the tents, the waiters will also serve "Radler," or shandy (a mixture of half beer and half lemon soda), as well as alcohol-free beer. Here's a tip: Make your first Mass a shandy.

Whether you are in the company of colleagues or friends, here's another important drinking rule to remember: Take it slow. Eating is essential. When you order the first beer, you should order something to eat at the same time. Keep in mind that a table reservation comes with one food coupon (worth at least 10 Euro) per person.

Yet another important Oktoberfest rule is not to be stingy with tips. The waiters work very hard, often carrying ten or twelve full-liter mugs of beer through the swaying crowds, and balancing trays laden with 18 chickens from one end of the tent to the other. Be generous—the servers really do appreciate it.

Friendly toasting

When the refrain "Prosit der Gemütlichkeit" sounds (which seems to happen about every seven minutes!), go along with it and clink glasses with your neighbors. It's part of the experience, and you can take small sips if you prefer. When clinking glasses, look the other person in the eye, and hold your beer mug by the handle—don't use your thumb and palm as you do when drinking, or you may get your fingers squashed.

A bad habit that's becoming more common is drinking before the fair, either to get into the spirit of things more quickly or because bottled beer is cheap compared with a Mass at the beer tents. Just keep in mind your limits and make smart choices.

Flirting at the Oktoberfest

Many people come to the Oktoberfest with the intention of finding romance. In fact, many a marriage has had its beginnings at the fair! With plenty of good beer and good conversation flowing in the tents, the Oktoberfest can be one of the best places to meet people from all around the world. Lasting friendships, also, can develop over a Mass or two.

Visiting the fair with your partner can be a lot of fun. For singles, though, it's high flirt-alert! Women dressed in dirndls should definitely make use of the bows of their aprons to send clear signals (see p. 23). A bow tied on the right means "I am already spoken for," but a bow tied on the left means "I'm single—and may be happy to accept a compliment or two from you."

"Bear in mind these few simple rules and tricks to get the most out of your evening…"

It's better not to:

· bid for an Oktoberfest table from an unreliable source on the Internet

· rent your outfit from a carnival-costume rental company, if you're going for an authentic look

· be a cheapskate when tipping

· address the waitress as "Zenzi"

· smoke in a beer tent

· pronounce the word "Mass" with a long instead of a short "a"

· hold a beer mug with two hands when drinking from it

· climb onto the table instead of the bench to dance

· argue with the security guards

· fall asleep at the table

· let yourself be provoked by drunks, or get into a fight

· steal a beer glass

· pee where it's not allowed

· "sleep it off" outdoors near Theresienhöhe

Bavarian potato salad

Potato salad makes a good accompaniment for many Bavarian dishes; it is also really good on its own. Depending on seasonal availability, try adding endive, celery root, or even chanterelle mushrooms.

Serves 4 · Prep time: 25 minutes · Marinating time: 20 minutes

1¾lb (750g) yellow potatoes, such as Yukon Gold
salt
¼ cup vegetable oil
1 onion, peeled and finely diced
3 tbsp white wine vinegar
1 cup vegetable broth
1 tbsp medium-hot mustard
pepper
2 tbsp chopped chives

1. Boil the potatoes, unpeeled, in salted water for about 20 minutes, or until cooked. Drain, allow the steam to evaporate, and peel. Set the potatoes aside to cool a little, then cut them into slices and put them in a bowl.

2. Heat the oil in a pan and sauté the onion. Add the vinegar and vegetable broth, stir in the mustard, and bring to a boil. Pour the hot marinade over the sliced potatoes and toss gently. Season the potato salad with salt and pepper and leave to marinate for about 20 minutes.

3. Sprinkle chives over the potato salad. Serve with dishes such as pork schnitzel cordon bleu (see p. 43), beer battered fish (see p. 78), or Oktoberfest chicken (see p. 74).

Variations
Prepare the potato salad as described above, but don't sprinkle it with chives. Instead, stir in one of the following:

Potato and endive salad
Slice ¼ of a head of endive into strips and stir into the potato salad.

Potato and celery root salad
Peel ½ of a celery root and cut it into bite-size pieces. Blanch the celery in boiling salted water and stir into the sliced potatoes. Leave to marinate for 20 minutes.

Potato salad with chanterelles and bacon
Heat 1 tbsp vegetable oil in a pan. Add 5½oz (150g) of diced smoked bacon and sauté until crisp. Add 7oz (200g) of chanterelle mushrooms and sauté. Season with salt and pepper, and stir into the potato salad.

Pretzel cheese sticks, snails, and chestnuts

You can't make the big Oktoberfest pretzels easily at home, but pretzel cheese sticks, snails, and chestnuts are very easy to make and taste at least as good. Of course, you can also twist the dough into pretzels if you like.

Makes 8 pieces · Prep time: 1 hour · Rising time: 1 hour 30 minutes · Baking time: 15 minutes

For the dough
- 4⅓ cups all-purpose flour, plus more for the work surface
- ¾oz (20g) cake yeast or 1 tsp active dry yeast
- 1 pinch of sugar
- 2 tbsp vegetable oil
- salt
- 1 tbsp baking soda

For sprinkling
- 5½oz (150g) grated Swiss cheese
- coarse salt
- sesame seeds
- poppy seeds
- sunflower seeds

1. Sift the flour into a large mixing bowl and make a well in the center. If using cake yeast, crumble it into the well and add a pinch of the sugar and a little lukewarm water. Use active dry yeast in the same way. Combine with a fork, incorporating some flour from the sides of the well, to make a starter. Cover the bowl with a dish towel and leave to rise in a warm place for about 15 minutes.

2. Add the oil, salt, and about 1 cup of lukewarm water to the bowl and stir to combine. Then, using your hands, knead the dough on a floured work surface until smooth and elastic. Put in an oiled bowl, cover with a dish towel, and leave to rise in a warm place for about 1 hour.

3. Knead the dough once more and divide it into eight pieces. To make cheese pretzel sticks, form thick ropes about 6in (15cm) long and 2in (5cm) thick. To make pretzel snails, form thick ropes about 8in (20cm) long and 1in (3cm) thick and curl them up to make snail shapes. For chestnuts, roll the dough into balls.

5. Preheat the oven to 400°F (200°C). Line a baking tray with parchment paper and dust with flour. Arrange the pretzel cheese sticks, snails, and chestnuts on the baking tray. Cover the tray and leave to rise for 15 minutes.

6. Put 1 cup of water and the baking soda in a pot and bring to a boil. Brush the cheese sticks, snails, and chestnuts generously with the soda solution.

7. Make a cut in the cheese sticks lengthwise, open out a little, and sprinkle cheese into the cut. Slice a cross into the tops of the chestnuts. Sprinkle the chestnuts and the snails with salt, sesame, poppy, or sunflower seeds. Bake in the middle of the oven for about 15 minutes. Cheese sticks, snails, and chestnuts go well with beer, a Brotzeit platter (see p. 12), or Oktoberfest chicken (see p. 74).

Variation: For pretzels, roll the dough portions into ropes about 16in (40cm) long and 1in (3cm) thick. Shape into pretzels, brush with soda solution, and bake as above. The solution is harmless, but avoid contact with aluminum so you don't get an unwanted chemical reaction.

Sweet treats & baked goods

Strauben

Makes 10 pieces · Prep time: 50 minutes

3 tbsp unsalted butter
1 tbsp sugar
1 pinch of salt
1¼ cups all-purpose flour
4 eggs
oil, for deep frying
2 cups confectioners' sugar
3 tbsp rum

You will also need
a piping bag with a star nozzle

1 Put 1 cup of water, the butter, sugar, and the salt in a pot and bring to a boil. Add the flour all at once and stir immediately with a wooden spoon until smooth. Continue to stir vigorously on the stove until the dough forms a ball and a white film appears on the bottom of the pot. Remove from the stove and leave the dough to cool a little.

2 Cut out ten squares of parchment paper, about 4×4in (10×10cm). Stir the eggs into the dough one at a time. Fill the piping bag with the dough and pipe circles about 3in (8cm) in diameter onto each square of paper.

3 In a shallow pot, heat enough oil to deep-fry the dough. One after the other, slide the strauben off the paper and into the hot oil, paper side up, and fry for about 5 minutes, or until golden brown. Turn them over and fry on the other side for about 2 minutes, until cooked. Using a slotted spoon, lift the strauben out of the oil and drain on paper towels.

4 Stir together the confectioners' sugar and rum until smooth and use to glaze the strauben.

Tip: *This deep-fried treat made from choux pastry is traditionally made in fall and winter. You can also make the glaze with lemon juice instead of rum, or dust the strauben with confectioners' sugar.*

Quark donut balls

Makes 20 pieces · Prep time: 35 minutes

2 cups all-purpose flour
1 tsp baking powder, or ½ a packet
3 eggs
⅔ cup granulated sugar
9oz (250g) full-fat quark (alternatively, use a thick and creamy full-fat yogurt)
zest of ½ organic lemon
milk (as needed)
oil, for deep frying
1 tsp ground cinnamon

1 Mix together the flour and baking powder. Beat the eggs with half of the sugar until foamy. Stir in the flour mixture, quark, and lemon zest. If the dough is too firm, stir in a little milk.

2 In a shallow pan, heat up enough oil to deep-fry the dough. Using two tablespoons, shape small balls from the dough and drop them into the hot oil. Fry for about 5 minutes until golden brown on all sides. Using a slotted spoon, lift the balls out of the oil and onto paper towels to drain.

3 Stir together the remaining sugar and the cinnamon. Roll the hot quark balls in the mixture until they are completely covered.

Dessert dumplings
with a sweet honey crust

When their mouth-watering, sweet smell wafts over the fairgrounds or through the house, resistance is futile. These divine dumplings are best served with vanilla custard, ideally homemade.

Serves 12 · Prep time: 45 minutes · Rising time: 1 hour 15 minutes · Baking time: 50 minutes

4 cups all-purpose flour, plus more for the work surface
¾oz (20g) cake yeast or 1 tsp active dry yeast
½ cup granulated sugar
1 cup lukewarm milk, plus more for baking
½ cup unsalted butter, plus more for buttering the casserole dish
2 large eggs
zest of 1 organic lemon
3 tbsp honey

To serve
2 cups vanilla custard (from a packet mix or homemade, see tip)

1 Sift the flour into a large mixing bowl and make a well in the center. Crumble the cake yeast into the well and add a pinch of the sugar and a little of the lukewarm milk. Use active dry yeast in the same way. Combine with a fork, incorporating some flour from the sides of the well, to make a starter. Cover the bowl with a dish towel and leave to rise in a warm place for about 15 minutes.

2 Melt the butter. Add half of the butter, the remaining milk, half of the sugar, the eggs, and the lemon zest to the starter, and stir until the dough comes together. Using your hands, knead the dough on a floured work surface until smooth and elastic. Put into an oiled bowl, cover with a dish towel, and leave to rise in a warm place for about 1 hour.

3 Generously butter the sides of an ovenproof casserole dish. Put the remaining melted butter and sugar in a small pot and stir over low heat until caramelized and light brown in color. Remove from the stove and stir in the honey. Pour the caramel mixture into the casserole dish and set aside to cool.

4 Preheat the oven to 350°F (180°C). Knead the dough briefly, then divide into 12 pieces and shape each piece into a slightly flattened dumpling. Arrange the dumplings side by side on top of the caramel. Pour about ½ cup milk into the dish, cover it tightly with a lid or aluminum foil, and bake the dumplings in the middle of the oven for about 50 minutes. Remove the dumplings from the dish one at a time and turn over so the honey crust is on top. Serve with vanilla sauce (see tip).

Tip: To make vanilla sauce, bring 2 cups of milk to a boil in a pot. Slice open a vanilla bean, scrape out the seeds, and add both to the milk. Whisk together 6 egg yolks and 2 tablespoons of sugar in a bowl, then stir the hot milk slowly into the egg mixture. Pour back into the pot and, stirring constantly with a wooden spoon, heat to about 160°F (70°C). The sauce is ready when it coats the back of the wooden spoon and rose-shaped waves form when you blow on it. Immediately take it off the stove, pour through a fine mesh sieve, and serve.

Millirahmstrudel
with a classic filling

This juicy strudel actually originates in Vienna, but today it is an absolute classic at the Oktoberfest. It is delicious eaten warm or cold, and best accompanied by a large cup of coffee.

Serves 12 · Prep time: 45 minutes · Resting time: 30 minutes · Baking time: 45 minutes

For the dough
1 recipe strudel dough (see p. 85)
3 tbsp unsalted butter, plus more for the baking dish
flour for the work surface
1–2 handfuls of breadcrumbs

For the filling
3 eggs
½ cup softened unsalted butter
½ cup granulated sugar
1lb 2oz (500g) quark (alternatively, use a thick and creamy, plain, non-fat yogurt)
10½oz (300g) sour cream
zest of 1 organic lemon
½ cup raisins

For the glaze
2 eggs
1 cup milk
1 packet vanilla sugar or 1 tsp pure vanilla extract

1. Prepare the strudel dough as described on page 85. Leave to rest for 30 minutes.

2. Meanwhile, make the filling. Separate the eggs and beat the egg whites in a bowl until they form stiff peaks. In a separate bowl, beat the butter and sugar together until fluffy, then beat in the egg yolks one at a time. Stir in the quark, sour cream, lemon zest, and raisins. Fold in the beaten egg whites.

3. Preheat the oven to 350°F (180°C). Generously butter an ovenproof dish. Knead the dough again on a floured work surface and roll it out. Dust a dish towel with flour, place the sheet of dough on top, and stretch as thinly as possible with your hands to make a rectangle of about 16×24in (40×60cm).

4. Melt the butter and brush it on the sheet of dough, then sprinkle the dough with breadcrumbs. Spread the filling evenly over the dough, leaving a clear edge about 1in (3cm) wide. With the aid of the dish towel, and working from the long end, roll up the dough to form a strudel. Place the strudel on the baking dish, seam side down, and tuck the ends underneath.

5. To make the glaze, whisk the eggs with the milk and vanilla sugar or vanilla extract, and pour the mixture over the strudel. Bake the strudel in the middle of the oven for about 45 minutes. Remove from the oven and cut into twelve pieces. Serve warm from the oven, or cold.

French toast
with plum butter and cinnamon sugar

Originally, the Bavarian version of French toast, called "Bavesen," was served on farms only at the end of the work year, which fell at Candlemas (February 2). This was the day servants received the rest of their yearly pay and the farmers' wives prepared Bavesen as thanks for the hard work of the farm hands and serving maids. This sweet dish also tastes delicious during the Oktoberfest.

Serves 4 · Prep time: 25 minutes

8 day-old slices of white bread
¼ cup plum butter, or plum compote (see p. 124) if unavailable
2 large eggs
1 tbsp flour
1 cup milk
2 tbsp sugar
½ tsp ground cinnamon
clarified unsalted butter, for frying

1. Lay out four slices of bread on a board and spread each slice with 1 tablespoon of plum butter, or plum compote. Top with another slice of bread and press together lightly.

2. Whisk together the eggs and the flour in a shallow bowl. Pour the milk into a second shallow bowl. Mix together the sugar and cinnamon on another plate.

3. Heat a generous amount of clarified butter in a large pan. Dip both sides of each sandwich into the milk until well soaked. Then dip both sides into the egg mixture and transfer immediately to the hot butter in the pan. Fry for about 5 minutes on each side until golden brown. Lift out of the pan and drain on paper towels, then dredge the hot French toast in cinnamon sugar. Serve immediately.

Tip: French toast also tastes delicious when prepared with braided buns or whole wheat bread instead of white bread. For a different filling, you may like to try jam or banana slices.

# Fluffy Kaiserschmarrn
with plum compote

What's that delicious smell? Even when everyone has had their fill, there's always room for a few forkfuls of irresistible, freshly cooked Kaiserschmarrn, a topsy-turvy kind of pancake. You could even serve it as a main course!

Serves 4 as a main course or 6–8 as dessert · Prep time: 1 hour

For the plum compote
2¼lb (1kg) plums
¼ cup sugar
1 cinnamon stick
2 cloves

For the Kaiserschmarrn
1⅔ cups all-purpose flour
1 tbsp sugar
1 pinch of salt
1 cup milk
4 eggs
clarified unsalted butter, for frying
1 handful of raisins, soaked in rum for at least 1 hour
1 handful of slivered almonds
confectioners' sugar, to serve

1. To make the plum compote, cut the plums in half and pit them. Put the sugar and 3 tablespoons of water in a pot and heat, without stirring, until caramelized. Add the plums, cinnamon stick, and cloves, and bring to a boil.

2. Reduce the heat and simmer the plums for about 5 minutes, stirring occasionally, until the juice has thickened but the plums have not completely disintegrated. Remove the compote from the stove and set aside to cool.

3. To make the Kaiserschmarrn, combine the flour, sugar, and salt in a bowl. Add the milk and whisk to make a thick batter.

4. Separate the eggs and whip the egg whites in a big bowl until they form stiff peaks. Stir the yolks into the batter, then fold the batter into the egg whites.

5. Heat a little clarified butter in one large or two small pans. Pour the batter into the pan. Drain the raisins and sprinkle them over the batter, along with the slivered almonds. Reduce the heat and cook the pancake for about 10 minutes, or until golden brown underneath. Cover the pan if necessary. Carefully turn over the pancake and cook the other side until golden brown.

6. Remove the pan from the stove. Using two forks, tear the pancake into bite-size pieces. Dust generously with confectioners' sugar and return the pan to the stove. Caramelize the sugar over moderate heat, frequently turning the pancake pieces as you do so.

7. Remove the Kaiserschmarrn from the pan immediately. Arrange on four plates and dust with confectioners' sugar. Serve with plum compote.

Sweet treats & baked goods 127

Crêpes filled with hazelnut cream

Serves 4 · Prep time: 30 minutes · Resting time: 30 minutes

3 tbsp unsalted butter
1¼ cup all-purpose flour
1 pinch of salt
¾ cup milk
6 eggs
oil, for frying
hazelnut-and-chocolate spread (from the jar), for spreading

1. Melt the butter and leave to cool a little. Combine the flour and salt in a bowl. Add the milk and eggs, and whisk to make a thin batter. Stir in the melted butter, cover, and leave to rest for about 30 minutes.

2. Heat a little oil in a pan. Pour in a ladlefull of batter and tilt the pan to ensure the batter evenly coats the bottom of the pan. Fry the crêpe on each side until golden brown. Remove from the frying pan and keep warm. Repeat until the batter is used up—it should yield about eight very thin crêpes, depending on the size of the pan.

3. Spread the crêpes with hazelnut-and-chocolate spread and fold up. Serve immediately.

Tip: Crêpes are good with other sweet fillings, such as bananas, applesauce, cinnamon sugar, plum compote (see p. 124), jam, or confectioners' sugar. They are also delicious with savory fillings such as pesto, tomatoes, sheeps' milk cheese (feta), Swiss cheese, ham, spinach, or even Creamy wild mushroom stew (see p. 89).

Fresh waffles

Serves 4 · Prep time: 45 minutes

2 cups all-purpose flour
1 tsp baking powder
½ cup melted unsalted butter
¾ cup granulated sugar
1 tsp zest of an organic lemon
3 eggs
1 cup sparkling mineral water
oil, for frying
confectioners' sugar, for dusting

You will also need
a waffle iron

1. Combine the flour and baking powder in a bowl. Beat the butter, sugar, and lemon zest in a bowl until foamy. Stir in the eggs one at a time. Add the flour mixture and the sparkling water, and combine to make a smooth batter.

2. Turn on the waffle iron. Brush a little oil on the cooking surfaces. For each waffle, pour a small ladlefull of batter on the bottom half of the waffle iron. Close the lid and bake the waffle for about 5 minutes until crisp. Remove the waffle. Continue until the batter is used up. Lay out the waffles side by side on a wire rack, dust them with confectioners' sugar, and serve immediately.

Tip: Add a dollop of whipped cream to the freshly baked waffles and serve with fresh fruit, applesauce, plum compote (see p. 124), jam, or cinnamon sugar, to taste.

Candy apples
with nonpareil

People dress up to the nines when they go to the fair—the prettiest dirndl and the smartest lederhosen are taken out of the closet for the occasion. Even plain apples are all dressed up in bright red festive gowns.

Makes 12 · Prep time: 50 minutes · Cooling time: 1 hour

12 apples
2 cups granulated sugar
½ cup agave syrup
a few drops of red food coloring
3½oz (100g) colored nonpareil

You will also need
12 long wooden skewers

1. Wash and thoroughly dry the apples. Pierce each apple from the top through to the bottom with a wooden skewer. Chill the apples for at least 1 hour.

2. In a pot, stir together the sugar, agave syrup, and ⅔ cup water and cook over low heat for about 30 minutes until syrupy. Test the syrup by dropping a dribble of it into cold water. If the sugar hardens in the water and can be rolled into a firm ball, the candy syrup is ready. If not, cook the syrup for another 5 minutes and repeat the test. Add enough food coloring to turn the syrup a deep red and take the pot off the stove.

3. Scatter the nonpareil onto a large plate. Dip each chilled apple into the syrup once or twice, let drip briefly, and immediately roll the bottom half of the apple in the nonpareil. Finally, sit the apples on the nonpareil and leave to harden in a dry place for about 15 minutes.

4. Serve the candy apples as soon as possible—depending on the humidity, the candy coating will become sticky again after a few hours.

Tip: To make chocolate-dipped fruit, melt dark, milk, or white chocolate in a bain-marie or in a bowl set over a pan of simmering water. Skewer whole fruit—such as strawberries or grapes—or pieces of fruit—such as bananas, apples, pineapple, or mango—and dip them into the melted chocolate. Sprinkle to taste with chopped nuts or nonpareil. Leave to dry on a cake rack.

Candied almonds & mixed nuts

Makes 1¾lb (750g) · Prep time: 20 minutes

3½ cups almonds and mixed nuts (such as hazelnuts, walnuts, pecans, and peanuts)
1¼ cups granulated sugar
½ tsp ground cinnamon

1. Line a baking tray with parchment paper. Dry-roast the almonds and mixed nuts in a large pan over low heat, stirring all the time, until you can smell the scent of the roasted nuts.

2. Divide the sugar into thirds. Sprinkle a third of the sugar over the nuts and caramelize. Repeat this step with the second portion of sugar, and again with the last portion. Finally, stir in the cinnamon.

3. Immediately remove the candied nuts from the pan and spread them out on the lined baking tray. Leave to cool briefly and serve while still warm.

Almond and pistachio nougat

Makes 1lb 2oz (500g)· Prep time: 30 minutes · Drying time: 2 days · Keeps for: 3 weeks

3 egg whites
1 pinch of salt
1 cup granulated sugar
1 packet vanilla sugar, or 1 tsp pure vanilla extract
¼ cup honey
¾ cup almonds
⅓ cup pistachios
1¾oz (50g) mixed candied orange and lemon peel, finely diced

1. Put the egg whites and salt in a stainless steel bowl and beat until they form stiff peaks. Drizzle in the sugar and vanilla sugar, or vanilla extract, beating constantly, then add the honey and beat until the mixture is thick.

2. Place the bowl over a pan of simmering water. Beating constantly, heat the mixture to about 160°F (70°C). For best results, check the temperature using a thermometer, such as a candy thermometer. Then remove the bowl from the simmering water immediately.

3. Stir the almonds, pistachios, and candied peel into the egg whites. Line a deep pan, such as the oven dripping tray, with parchment paper and pour in the mixture. Leave to dry for at least 1 day.

4. Cover the nougat with parchment paper, put a cutting board on top, and weigh down with items like cans of food, for example. Leave the nougat to rest for at least 1 more day. It should be firm enough to cut, but still sticky.

5. Dip a knife in water and slice the nougat into rectangles or cubes. Serve right away or store in an airtight container, layered with parchment paper.

Glazed gingerbread
with aromatic spices

This type of gingerbread is called "Magenbrot" ("stomach bread") locally, as it is thought to be good for the digestion. A popular Oktoberfest treat, it is easy to make and keeps well.

Makes about 30 pieces · Prep time: 35 minutes · Baking time: 20 minutes · Resting time: 1 week · Keeps for: 3 weeks

For the dough
2 cups all-purpose flour
2 cups whole wheat rye flour
2 tsp baking powder, or 1 packet
1 cup granulated sugar
1 tsp ground cinnamon
1 pinch of ground cloves
1 large egg
1 cup milk

For the sugar glaze
1¼ cups granulated sugar
1 tbsp cocoa powder

1. Preheat the oven to 350°F (180°C). Line a baking tray with parchment paper. Combine both types of flour, the baking powder, sugar, cinnamon, and cloves. Add the egg and milk, and knead well to make a smooth dough. Shape the dough into three logs about 1½in (4cm) in diameter.

2. Place the logs on the baking tray and bake in the middle of the oven for about 20 minutes. Remove from the oven and, while still warm, cut the logs diagonally into slices about 1½in (4cm) thick.

3. To make the sugar glaze, bring the sugar, cocoa powder, and a scant ½ cup water to a boil in a pot. Working in batches, dip the rhombus-shaped gingerbread pieces into the glaze and put them on a cake rack to dry. If you like, dip a second time. Once the glaze has dried, layer the gingerbread in an airtight container and rest for 1 week before serving, to allow the flavors to develop.

Granatsplitter

These mini cakes are an elegant way of using up leftover baked goods such as cakes and cookies. For many fairgoers, they are a taste of happiness! They are best eaten straight out of the palm of your hand.

Makes 8 pieces · Prep time: 1 hour · Cooling time: 4 hours 30 minutes

For the dough
- 3 tbsp cold, unsalted, butter
- ¾ cup all-purpose flour, plus more for the work surface
- 2 tbsp sugar
- 1 large egg yolk

To make the filling and glaze
- ¼ cup cornstarch
- 1 tbsp cocoa powder
- 2 tbsp sugar
- 1 packet vanilla sugar or 1 tsp pure vanilla extract
- 1 cup milk
- 3 tbsp slivered almonds
- 7oz (200g) leftover cake and cookies
- 3½oz (100g) dark chocolate couverture (ready-made)
- 1 cup softened unsalted butter
- 1⅓fl oz (4cl) rum
- coconut flakes, for sprinkling

You will also need
- a round pastry cutter, about 2½in (6cm) in diameter

1. To make the dough, cut the butter into cubes. Mix together the flour and sugar, then add the butter, egg yolk, and about 3 tablespoons of cold water. Working quickly, knead to make a firm dough. Wrap the dough in plastic wrap and rest in the refrigerator for about 30 minutes.

2. Preheat the oven to 350°F (180°C). Line a baking tray with parchment paper. Roll out the dough on a floured work surface and cut out eight circles with the pastry cutter. Place the pastry rounds and the remaining dough cut-offs on the baking tray and bake in the middle of the oven for about 10 minutes, or until golden brown. Remove from the oven and leave to cool.

3. To make the filling, stir together the cornstarch, cocoa powder, sugar, and vanilla sugar or vanilla extract, and half the milk. Bring the remaining milk to a boil. Add the cornstarch mixture to the boiling milk and cook for about 2 minutes, stirring constantly, to make a thick, firm, pudding. Remove from the stove and leave to cool, stirring occasionally to prevent a skin forming.

4. Toast the slivered almonds in a pan, stirring constantly, until they are golden brown. Remove from the heat and set aside to cool. Crumble the leftover cake, cookies, and baked pastry remnants. Melt the chocolate couverture according to the instructions on the package.

5. Beat the butter until foamy. Stir in the pudding 1 tablespoonful at a time. Add the cake, cookie, and pastry crumbs, slivered almonds, and rum, and stir together to make a creamy mixture. Pour into a freezer bag, snip off one of the corners, and pipe onto the pastry rounds to make a tower shape. Pour the chocolate couverture over the cakes and immediately sprinkle with coconut flakes.

6. Refrigerate the cakes for about 4 hours before serving. These are perfect with a cup of coffee.

Gingerbread hearts
decorated with sugar icing

Simple messages such as "Greetings from the Oktoberfest," "I love you," or "Kiss me" are just some of the multitude of gingerbread heart inscriptions you may come across at the fair. These homemade heart-shaped gingerbread cookies are perfect for giving away, keeping for yourself, or to create the Oktoberfest look at home!

Makes 4 hearts · Prep time: 1 hour (plus 1 hour inactive time) · Chilling time: 8 hours · Baking time: 15 minutes

For the dough
½ cup unsalted butter
¾ cup honey
1½ cup brown sugar
4¾ cups all-purpose flour, plus more for the work surface
1 tbsp cocoa powder
2 tsp ground cinnamon
1 tsp ground ginger
½ tsp ground allspice
½ tsp ground anise seed
½ tsp ground cardamom
½ tsp ground coriander
¼ tsp ground cloves
¼ tsp grated nutmeg
1½ tsp baking soda
1 large egg

For the sugar icing
2 egg whites
3⅓ cups confectioners' sugar
various food colors (to taste)

You will also need
1 heart-shaped cardboard template, about 8in (20cm) across
small freezer bag
colored ribbons

1 For the dough, combine the butter, honey, and sugar in a pot over medium heat and bring to a boil, stirring constantly, then remove from the stove and leave to cool.

2 Combine the flour, cocoa, spices, and baking soda in a bowl. Stir the egg into the butter mixture. Add the butter mixture to the flour, then knead to make a smooth dough. Wrap in plastic wrap and put into the refrigerator to rest for at least 8 hours.

3 Remove the dough from the refrigerator and let it come to room temperature (this will take about an hour). Preheat the oven to 350°F (180°C). Line two baking trays with parchment paper. Turn out the dough onto a floured work surface and roll out to about the thickness of a finger. Using the template, cut out four hearts from the dough and place two on each baking tray. Bake in the middle of the oven for about 15 minutes, then remove from the oven and leave to cool.

4 To make the sugar icing, beat the egg whites until they form soft peaks. Gradually beat in the sifted confectioners' sugar to make a thick icing. Use the food colors to make different colored icing and spoon each color into a small freezer bag. Snip a small corner off each bag, then use to pipe words and decorations onto the gingerbread hearts. Leave to dry for about 30 minutes.

5 If you like, make two holes in the top of each heart, thread with enough ribbon to hang around your neck, and tie the ends in a knot.

Where, when, what, how: a brief visitors' guide to the fair

Where can I stay during the fair?
No matter where you stay during the Oktoberfest, rule number one is planning ahead! Book your hotel room at least a year in advance. To rent an apartment, keep an eye out on the Internet early on. Munich is fully booked during the fair, and the prices go up with demand. Camping is a good alternative if you like to be close to nature and don't need luxury or peace and quiet. The popular city campground in München-Thalkirchen, right on the Isar river, is beautifully located but very busy during the Oktoberfest. You can do as many visitors do and rent an RV for a few days; if you choose this option, it is advisable to rent a space in the dedicated Oktoberfest campgrounds in München-Riem. If you are really lucky, you have friends in Munich who have a spare bed and are happy to join you for a tour of the Oktoberfest.

When should I go to the fair?
You can experience the fair in very different ways at different times. When you enjoy it most will depend on who you are going with and what you plan to do. In general, it is quietest during the week until midafternoon. After about 3pm, more and more visitors arrive at the tents, among them many companies with their employees or customers. The party really gets going after 6pm, when the bands start to play the Oktoberfest hits—until then, things are more low-key.

If you are looking for calm Bavarian "Gemütlichkeit," you will not find it on a Saturday. On Saturdays, the huge crowds barely make any progress between one ride and the next, and often the tents close early in the morning due to overcrowding. Avoid Saturdays if at all possible, especially if you are a first-time visitor, or you may get the wrong impression and be disappointed. Saturdays on the fairgrounds are generally unsuitable for families with children—in fact, strollers are not permitted on the fairgrounds on Saturdays at all.

How can I reserve a table?
Even Munich residents dream of having a table reserved at the fair! Unfortunately, simply picking up the phone and booking ahead, as you would do with a restaurant, does not work. Your best bet is to contact your chosen festival tent landlord six to eight months before the fair, either by letter, by fax, or by online form. Information about how to reserve a table can be found on the festival tent's website. Without exception, you will need to get together ten of you to make a reservation—this is the number of people who fit around a beer table. And then you will need to be patient—and lucky: There is no reservation guarantee. If you have been successful, a letter of confirmation—giving the date, time, and table number—will be sent out to you around the end of February. Remember that reservations are limited to a specific time slot, so if you have snagged one of the coveted table reservations, it is absolutely essential that you and everyone else in your party turn up on time for your designated slot.

How do I get to the fair and back?
Two-thirds of all visitors travel to the fair by S-Bahn or U-Bahn (Munich's two train networks). You have a choice of four train stations. The main station for the fair, Theresienwiese, is often overcrowded. Alternatively, get off at S-Bahn station Hackerbrücke or U-Bahn stations Goetheplatz or Poccistraße. From these stations, it takes only about ten minutes to walk to the nearest fairground entrance. Taxis and privately-owned rickshaws are also popular. If you are really only going to drink one "Radler" or shandy, come by bicycle, which can be conveniently parked right in front of the

fairgrounds. Driving a car to get there and back, however, is not a good idea at all. The police are out in force during the Oktoberfest, plus you'll have a hard time finding parking. A good option for many is to go by train and return by taxi. This way, you can avoid the drunken train crowds on your way home.

Is Bavarian traditional costume really mandatory?
No, but a proper traditional outfit can significantly increase the fun factor. But before you spend money in some dubious store near the main train station on (artificial) leather shorts (that are made in China), or on an ill-fitting, cheap dirndl that won't survive the first evening, rest assured: Regular clothes are fine, too. You will want to be comfortable.

What is the best spot for watching the Grand Entry and the Costume and Riflemen's Procession?
Both parade routes go through the city center. The Grand Entry of the Oktoberfest Landlords and Breweries on Saturday takes a shorter route along Sonnenstraße and Schwanthalerstraße to the fairgrounds. The Costume and Riflemen's Procession, which lasts about three hours in total, begins on Maximilianstraße at the Isar river, continues past the Residenz and Odeonsplatz, along Brienner Straße to Sonnenstraße and then on to the fairgrounds, so these roads are closed to traffic for the parade. If you want to sit to watch the parade, you'll have to purchase tickets. Seating stands are set up along the entire parade route. Tickets can be purchased in advance (for example from Munich Ticket) at a cost of around 35 Euro. Standing room is free, but you will need to be at your chosen spot early, and be sure to wear comfortable shoes and warm clothes.

Where can I go to continue celebrating in Oktoberfest style after the tents have closed?
Fair after-parties have been trendy in Munich for several years. They are held everywhere in the city—though mostly not too far from the fairgrounds—in bars, pubs, clubs, and sometimes also in spaces not usually used as party venues, until 3am or later. But seasoned fairgoers tend to go straight home in order to rest for the next day's activities. Whichever you choose, have fun!

A phrase guide to beer-tent Bavarian

Even if many Munich residents no longer speak the Bavarian dialect, the fair is a traditional Bavarian festival. You will definitely get to know some locals, so communication problems are almost inevitable. For those who don't want to miss a thing in the sociable atmosphere of the tents, we can provide a little help. This glossary of phrases will prepare you for some standard phrases used at the Oktoberfest. Along with the oft-heard *"Oans, zwoa, gsuffa!"* ("One, two, bottoms up!"), the following expressions will come in handy:

In the beer tent

A Mass und ein Hendl, biddschön	A Mass (liter) of beer and half a chicken, please
(I kriagat) no oane	I'd like another Mass
Oane geht no	I can handle one more Mass (at least, I think so)
Kracherl	carbonated lemon soda
Mongtratzerl	A small appetizer. Also often used to complain about a portion that is too small ("Des war ja nur a Mongtratzerl" = "That was just a mongtratzerl")
Stamperl	a schnaps glass or a glass of schnaps (i.e. the contents)
I konn nimma	I'm (more than) full
lack	stale, no longer sparkling (beer, sodas)
Schwoam mas obi!	Let's empty our mugs! and also, Let's have a beer, instead of arguing!
Noagerl	A little bit of beer left at the bottom of the beer mug
Noagerlzuzler	Someone who nurses his or her beer and doesn't order a fresh one
Sauf di zamm!	Drink up!

Starting and ending a conversation

Servus/Griaß di	Greeting someone
Servus/Griaßts eich	Greeting several/many people
Is do no frei?	Is this seat unoccupied?
Hock di hera, rutsch ma zamm	We'll make room for you and move a bit closer together
Hock di hera, samma mehra	Popular jocular saying that means the same thing as above
fei	A difficult-to-translate expression generally used to strengthen a statement ("Des beer is fei guat" = "This beer is actually really good")
Mei, ham mir a Gaudi!	We're having fun here, aren't we!
Wos bleast denn so?	You don't need to shout, I can hear you very well
Eam/sie schaug oo!	Depending on the situation, either an admiring or a disrespectful comment about what someone has just said or done ("Eam" for males, "Sie" for females)

Interpersonal encounters

Gschpusi	male or female companion, friend, lover, or mistress
Deandl	this usually doesn't refer to a dirndl dress, but a young girl
obandln	flirting, chatting somebody up
I mog di	I find you attractive and would like to get to know you better
Du bist a ganz a scheena Fega	a compliment paid to a (young) lady, one you don't want to burn your fingers on, although she is attractive
Deaf i dia a Busserl gebm?	May I kiss you? (a "Busserl" is a short kiss on the cheek or mouth)
gwampert	fat, with a large stomach
Grischperl	a weedy man
Bazi	swindler, a scheming fellow
Gschaftlhuaba	someone who is very full of themselves
Preiß	a visitor who speaks high German
Saupreiß	a disagreeable visitor who speaks high German
oide Zausl	term for an older man who behaves in an undignified way
oide Dackl	term for an older man with an excessive interest in women
Spinatwachtl	swear word for an older, slightly eccentric lady
bleede Hena	mild swear word for a woman who has aroused disapproval
Schaug, dassd weidakimmst/ Geh, schleich di!	It's better if you leave (slither off) right away
Mogsd a Schelln/Watschn/Fotzn?	I'm going to clobber you in a minute!
Nimm deine Bratzn (do) weg!	You are getting too close/get off!
Sei hoid ned so zwieda!	Why are you so unfriendly?

In front of and behind the tent, and on the way home

Ziegarn	cigar, smoked behind the tent
Drah ma no a Rundn	Let's take another stroll over the fairgrounds
Guadln	candies
Heb di (bei mia) ei!	Hold on to my arm! (in cases where someone is a little wobbly or needs some help after leaving a beer tent)
I wui hoam	I want to go home
Mia is ned guad/I muaß speibm/ Mia draat si ois	I'm feeling unwell / I'm going to be sick / I'm dizzy
I geh amoi aufs Haisl!	I'm going for a quick visit to the bathroom
wuid biesln	not seeking out the proper sanitary facilities to urinate / urinating in public
Pfiat di/eana!	Bye-bye!
Wia schaugts aus, seng ma uns wieda?	Will we be seeing each other again?

Index

Recipe index

A/B
almond and pistachio nougat 131
arugula spread 12
autumnal squash soup with pumpkin seed oil 28
Bavarian cabbage 99
Bavarian cabbage slaw 100
Bavarian chicken hash with fresh vegetables 73
Bavarian potato salad 110
Bavarian sausage salad 18
beef roulades stuffed with dill pickles and bacon 61
beef soup with noodles (tip) 57
beer battered fish with remoulade sauce 78
boiled beef with fresh horseradish 57
boiled ham hocks on a bed of sauerkraut 44
braised lamb shanks on root vegetables 66
bread dumplings 104
Brotzeit platter with cheese, cold meats, radish, and more 12

C/D
cabbage slaw, Bavarian 100
Camembert spread 12
candied almonds & mixed nuts 131
candy apples with nonpareil 128
carrot and cabbage slaw 100
char, pan-fried, with lemon-and-parsley butter 77
cheese sticks (mini pretzels) 113
chestnuts (mini pretzels) 113
chicken, Oktoberfest 74
chocolate-dipped fruit (tip) 128
classic mashed potatoes 103
clear chicken soup with noodles and vegetables 34
cordon rouge, pork schnitzel (variation) 43
creamy Savoy cabbage with fried eggs 97
creamy wild mushroom stew 89
crêpes filled with hazelnut cream 127
crispy duck with apple and onion stuffing 70
dessert dumplings with a sweet honey crust 119
duck, crispy, with apple and onion stuffing 70

F
fish, beer battered, with remoulade sauce 78
fish grilled on a stick (tip) 77
fluffy Kaiserschmarrn with plum compote 124
French toast with plum butter and cinnamon sugar 123
fresh waffles 127
freshly smoked trout fillets 20
fruit, chocolate-dipped (tip) 128

G
gingerbread hearts decorated with sugar icing 136
glazed gingerbread with aromatic spices 132
goulash, hearty, with Oktoberfest beer 33
Granatsplitter 135
gravad lax sandwiches with homemade cured salmon 25
Grünkern (spelt) patties with paprika 94

H
ham hocks, boiled, on sauerkraut 44
ham hocks, roast (tip) 74
head cheese, tart 18
hearty goulash with Oktoberfest beer 33
homemade liverwurst with nutmeg and marjoram 15

K/L
Kaiserschmarrn, fluffy, with plum compote 124
lamb shanks, braised, on root vegetables 66
leberkaese 49
leek and potato soup with pretzel croutons 38
liver dumpling soup with chopped chives 37
liverwurst, homemade, in a screw-top jar 15
lung stew 62

M/N
matjes herring fillets in a creamy apple-and-yogurt sauce 27
Millirahmstrudel with a classic filling 120
Milzwurst 49
mixed salad with deep-fried Camembert 16
nougat, almond and pistachio 131

O/P/Q
Oktoberfest chicken 74
pan-fried char with lemon-and-parsley butter 77
parslied potatoes 103
poached pear halves filled with cranberry sauce (tip) 65
pork, roast (tip) 47
pork sausage 49
pork schnitzel cordon bleu 43
potato and celery root salad (variation) 110
potato and endive salad (variation) 110
potato chip spirals with two kinds of dips 86
potato dumplings 104
potatoes, classic mashed 103
potatoes, parslied 103
potato salad, Bavarian 110
potato salad with chanterelles and bacon (variation) 110

pretzel cheese sticks, snails, and chestnuts 113
pretzels (variation) 113
Quark donut balls 116

R
radish spread 12
ravioli, vegetable-stuffed, with fried onions 106
red cabbage 99
remoulade sauce 78
roast pork (tip) 47
roast ham hocks (tip) 74
roast suckling pig with onion stuffing 47

S
salad, mixed, with deep-fried Camembert 16
sauerbraten, tender, in red wine sauce 58
sauerkraut 44
sauerkraut strudel 85
sausage salad, Bavarian 18
sausage salad, Swiss 18
Savoy cabbage, creamy, with fried eggs 97
Schweinswürstel 49
snails (mini pretzels) 113
spaetzle (variation) 82
spinach spaetzle with fried onions 82
squash soup, autumnal, with pumpkin seed oil 28
Steckerlfisch (tip) 77
Strauben 116
stuffed breast of veal 54
suckling pig, roast, with onion stuffing 47
Swiss sausage salad 18

T
tart head cheese 18
tender sauerbraten in red wine sauce 58
trout fillets, freshly smoked 20

V/W
vanilla sauce (tip) 119
veal sausage 49
veal, stuffed breast of 54
vegetable-stuffed ravioli with fried onions 106
venison stew in juniper and red wine sauce 65
waffles, fresh 127
Weißwurst 49
wild mushroom stew, creamy 89
Wollwurst 49

Subject index

A/B/C
accommodation 138
Armbrustschützen tent 31, 51
Augustiner tent 31, 50, 68
beer 8, 30, 50, 51, 52, 68, 108, 109
beer mug 108, 109
beer price 51
beer tents 7, 8, 30, 31, 92, 138
bow 23, 108
Bräurosl 31, 50
breweries 8, 30, 50–51
camping 138
charivari 22

D/F
daytime fair 53
dirndl 22, 139, 141
dirndl aprons 22, 108
Ferris wheel 91
Fischer-Vroni 7, 31, 50, 52

G/H/I
Grand Entry 68, 139
Hacker tent 31, 50, 68
Herzkasperl tent 31, 50, 92
Hofbräu tent 31, 51
hotel rooms 138
Italian weekend 69

K/L/M
Käfer's gourmet tent 31, 51
Kettenkarussell 91
Krinoline 90
Kuffler's Weinzelt 31
landlords 8, 30, 53, 68, 138, 139
leather shorts 22, 139
lederhosen 22, 139
Löwenbräu tent 31, 51
lunch specials 53
Marstall tent 31, 51
Mass 52, 68, 108, 109, 140
Münchner Kindl 68
music 30, 90

O/R/S
Ochsenbraterei 31, 51, 52
Old Fair 7, 31, 50, 92
"O'zapft is!" 8, 68
"Radler" (shandy) 61, 108
reservations 31, 108, 138
rides 90, 91, 92, 138
Schichtl 90
Schottenhamel 8, 31, 51, 68
Schützen tent 31, 51
shandy 61, 108
swing ride 91, 92

T/W
Teufelsrad 90
Theresienwiese 7, 8, 68, 138
tipping 108, 109
Toboggan 90
Tradition tent 31, 50, 92
traditional costume 22, 69, 109, 139
waiters 30, 69
Winzerer Fähndl 31, 51

Acknowledgments

Jasmin Blanda, thank you for the super food styling assistance and your work as a hand model; Team Block K, thank you to the world's best service team—Martina Bendig, Daniela Geisenberger, Susanne Haas, Sonja Herpich, Eva Ludwig and Andrea Wellmann-Burk—in the Hofbräu tent; DK, thank you for making this book a reality; Stefan Hempl and Hofbräu Munich, thank you for the generous support with beer, props, and plenty of room for taking photographs; Rudi Herpich, thank you, you clever Bavarian man and first-class model; Marianne Kranz, thank you for the fabulous dirndl dresses (www.exklusive-tracht.de); Eva Probst, thank you for the excellent Bavarian sausages and the absolutely top-quality meat (www.metzgerei-probst.de); Michaela Schifferl and Tobias Martl, thank you for decorating all those gingerbread hearts; Feline Skowronek, thank you to our favorite model; Brigitte Sporrer, thank you for the wonderful photographs in this book; the Steinberg family, thank you for 20 shared years at the fair; Martin Widmann and HB Logistik, thank you for the beautiful decommissioned beer tables for the photographs (www.schanktec.de).

Julia Skowronek, trained cook, Münchner by choice, food stylist, and author, lives in Munich. The Bavarian cuisine and the "Wiesn" are particularly close to her heart. She has also worked for 20 years as a waiter in the Hofbräu tent during the Oktoberfest.

Food photographer Brigitte Sporrer was born in Munich and still lives there. The beauty of Bavarian food and culinary culture are very clear to her. She has contributed images to several cookbooks.

Recipes and food styling Julia Skowronek
Feature text Katja Treu
Translation Barbara Hopkinson
Photography Brigitte Sporrer
Editor Petra Teetz
US Editors Allison Singer, Rebecca Warren
Graphic design and illustrations Silke Klemt

For DK Verlag:
Publishing manager Monika Schlitzer
Managing editor Sarah Fischer
Production manager Dorothee Whittaker
Production Sophie Schiela
Production coordinator Katharina Dürmeier

First American Edition, 2015
Published in the United States by DK Publishing
345 Hudson Street, New York, New York 10014

Copyright © 2015 Dorling Kindersley Limited
A Penguin Random House Company
15 16 17 18 19 10 9 8 7 6 5 4 3 2 1
001–284578–August/2015

All rights reserved. Without limiting the rights under the copyright reserved above, no part of this publication may be reproduced, stored in or introduced into a retrieval system, or transmitted, in any form, or by any means (electronic, mechanical, photocopying, recording, or otherwise), without the prior written permission of the copyright owner. Published in Great Britain by Dorling Kindersley Limited.

A catalog record for this book is available from the Library of Congress. ISBN 978-1-4654-3939-0

DK books are available at special discounts when purchased in bulk for sales promotions, premiums, fund-raising, or educational use. For details, contact: DK Publishing Special Markets, 345 Hudson Street, New York, New York 10014 SpecialSales@dk.com

Printed and bound in Hong Kong

All images © Dorling Kindersley Limited
For further information see: www.dkimages.com

A WORLD OF IDEAS:
SEE ALL THERE IS TO KNOW

www.dk.com